TO:

....

FROM:

....

DATE:

....

DEVOTIONS
TO CULTIVATE
A TEEN GIRL'S
FAITH

HILARY BERNSTEIN

SEEN

DEVOTIONS TO CULTIVATE A TEEN GIRL'S FAITH

© 2022 by Barbour Publishing, Inc.

Print ISBN 979-8-89151-107-1

All rights reserved. No part of this publication may be reproduced or transmitted for commercial purposes, except for brief quotations in printed reviews, without written permission of the publisher. Reproduced text may not be used on the World Wide Web. No Barbour Publishing content may be used as artificial intelligence training data for machine learning, or in any similar software development.

Churches and other noncommercial interests may reproduce portions of this book without the express written permission of Barbour Publishing, provided that the text does not exceed 500 words or 5 percent of the entire book, whichever is less, and that the text is not material quoted from another publisher. When reproducing text from this book, include the following credit line: "From *Seen: Devotions to Cultivate a Teen Girl's Faith*, published by Barbour Publishing, Inc. Used by permission."

Scripture quotations marked NIV are taken from THE HOLY BIBLE, NEW INTERNATIONAL VERSION®. NIV®. Copyright © 1973, 1978, 1984, 2011 by Biblica, Inc.® Used by permission. All rights reserved worldwide.

Scripture quotations marked ESV are from The ESV® Bible (The Holy Bible, English Standard Version®). ESV® Text Edition: 2016. Copyright © 2001 by Crossway, a publishing ministry of Good News Publishers. The ESV® text has been reproduced in cooperation with and by permission of Good News Publishers. Unauthorized reproduction of this publication is prohibited. All rights reserved.

Scripture quotations marked NLT are taken from the *Holy Bible*, New Living Translation copyright © 1996, 2004, 2015 by Tyndale House Foundation. Used by permission of Tyndale House Publishers, Inc. Carol Stream, Illinois 60188. All rights reserved.

Scripture quotations marked TLB are taken from The Living Bible copyright © 1971 by Tyndale House Foundation. Used by permission of Tyndale House Publishers Inc., Carol Stream, Illinois 60188. All rights reserved. The Living Bible, TLB, and the The Living Bible logo are registered trademarks of Tyndale House Publishers.

Published by Barbour Publishing, Inc., 1810 Barbour Drive, Uhrichsville, Ohio 44683, www.barbourbooks.com

Our mission is to inspire the world with the life-changing message of the Bible.

Printed in China.

YOUR LOVING HEAVENLY FATHER SEES YOU, GIRL!

And not only does He see you, but He understands you too.

Your disappointments, joys, heartaches, secrets. . . *everything*—He sees it all, and He loves you. *Every. Single. Part. Of. You.*

These 180 devotions and inspiring prayers, each one rooted in biblical truth, will reassure your young heart. With each turn of the page, you'll come to trust that God truly gets you—even when no one else does—because you're His! You belong to Him!

Spend daily quiet time meditating on these devotions in the presence of the God who sees you and be encouraged as your heart and soul are comforted by His never-ending love and grace.

The Lord gazes down upon mankind from heaven where he lives. He has made their hearts and closely watches everything.

Psalm 33:13–15 TLB

CHOSEN!

As God's chosen people, holy and dearly loved, clothe yourselves with compassion, kindness, humility, gentleness and patience.

Colossians 3:12 NIV

Everyone knows the thrill of being chosen, whether it's being picked for a team, making a cast list, getting accepted to a program, or simply being chosen as a friend. And everyone knows the agony of defeat. Rejection hurts.

The amazing news is that through Jesus Christ, God has chosen you. You're on His team. You've made His list. You're part of His program. You didn't earn this favor through your talents and abilities. It doesn't matter what you look like or who your family is or isn't. He chose you. *You!*

The fact that the God of the universe chose you is amazingly special. He loves you dearly. Because of the way He set you apart to be His own, you should act differently. Represent Him with a humble and kind life filled with gentleness, patience, and compassion. You're chosen by the Lord God Almighty. Out of His overflowing love, He picked you. It's time to live like it!

Lord Almighty, thank You for choosing me! Please help me represent You with love and kindness.

FINDING THE GOOD

I trust in your unfailing love; my heart rejoices in your salvation. I will sing the LORD's praise, for he has been good to me.

PSALM 13:5–6 NIV

You know that feeling when something really good happens to you and you just can't wait to tell someone else? When we think about what God has done for us and really consider it, we can experience that same amazingly happy feeling.

He loves you so very much just for being you. His love doesn't fail. It doesn't stop; it doesn't change; it is not dependent on you and your moods or His moods.

Think about something or someone you love the most. Then take that love and multiply it by a million. He loves you even more than that. To know you mean that much to God is pretty amazing. And it's something to get excited about!

When you experience God's love, tell Him! Thank Him. Praise Him. And don't be shy about telling other people about the really good things He's doing in you and for you.

Father, I praise You for the amazing way You work in my life! Thank You for Your love.

CHILDLIKE FAITH

Then Jesus called for the children and said to the disciples, "Let the children come to me. Don't stop them! For the Kingdom of God belongs to those who are like these children."

LUKE 18:16 NLT

For most of your life, you've probably either heard someone tell you to grow up or told yourself you need to act older. Even though growing up and maturing is a natural part of life and a good thing, Jesus taught that believers should have childlike faith.

Having *childlike* faith doesn't mean having a *childish* faith, but it does mean you don't need to have everything figured out. And that's good news, because there's no way to figure everything out!

What you need is to believe like a child. You need a simple faith that's based completely on trust. You don't need to comprehend all the nitty-gritty details. Instead, you can run to Jesus at any time for any reason. You can come to Him!

Father, thank You for knowing my heart. You know my faith in You. I don't need a bunch of deep, theological answers. I just need to know and trust Jesus.

SEE YOUR BLESSINGS

The Lord is my chosen portion and my cup; you hold my lot. The lines have fallen for me in pleasant places; indeed, I have a beautiful inheritance. I bless the Lord who gives me counsel; in the night also my heart instructs me.

Psalm 16:5–7 ESV

If and when you put your trust in Christ, God pours out His blessings on you. He gives you a precious inheritance—eternity with Him! He makes things work out in your favor, as He's continually watching over you and protecting you. He guides and directs you during the day when you're listening for Him and even in the night when you don't realize it.

Our Lord isn't a stingy miser. Quite the contrary, He loves to give good gifts to those He loves. Once you're part of His family through Jesus, He definitely loves you. When you notice all the big and small ways He's showing His care with His good gifts, make sure to thank Him!

Father God, thank You for loving me so much that You give me really good gifts and plan wonderful things for me. You are so very good to me!

THE POWER OF GOD

Although he was crucified in weakness, he now lives by the power of God. We, too, are weak, just as Christ was, but when we deal with you we will be alive with him and will have God's power.

2 Corinthians 13:4 NLT

If you would make a list of all your strengths and weaknesses, chances are it would be easy to pick yourself apart and pinpoint all your failures and flaws.

Even if we wish we could be perfect in something, imperfection is part of this life. Weakness is something absolutely everyone deals with, even though each person has very different strengths and very different weaknesses.

When you trust Christ as your Lord and Savior, you receive a lot of great gifts, like forgiveness and forever life. You'll also be filled with God's power. You still might feel weak, but with Him working through you, you'll be strong. His power and strength will be part of you as you learn to rely on Him.

Father, Your power is totally amazing. Thank You for sharing it with me! I may be weak, but You'll make me strong.

WAITING IN HOPE

We wait in hope for the Lord; he is our help and our shield. In him our hearts rejoice, for we trust in his holy name. May your unfailing love be with us, Lord, even as we put our hope in you.

Psalm 33:20–22 niv

Waiting can seem so very hard! Whether you're waiting on something that you're really looking forward to or waiting for something uncomfortable to be over, patience is really difficult!

When things in this world make you feel out of sorts—you might feel scared or worried or angry about things that are happening now or might happen in the future—patience seems almost impossible. Yet when you step back and remember who God is, it's possible to wait in hope. He is your help! He is your protective shield of defense. His name and His character are worthy of your trust. Because His love never fails, you can rejoice in Him and wait for Him.

Father, I may not like waiting, but I'm really glad I can wait in hope for You. Please help me patiently wait for You to work out Your very good plans.

OUT OF THE DARK

But you are a chosen people, a royal priesthood, a holy nation, God's special possession, that you may declare the praises of him who called you out of darkness into his wonderful light. Once you were not a people, but now you are the people of God; once you had not received mercy, but now you have received mercy.

1 PETER 2:9–10 NIV

When you consider all that God has done for you and how highly He thinks of you, it's pretty amazing. He has called you out of darkness into His wonderful light. He has chosen you to be His own. In His eyes, you're royal (You're now the daughter of the King of kings!) and holy. He has poured out mercy on you so that you receive so much more goodness and grace and forgiveness than you deserve. On top of all of that, He looks at you as His special possession.

That kind of goodness should give you a reason to praise Him! He knows exactly who you are and what you do and still thinks you're special!

Father, You are so very good to me! Thank You for choosing me and adopting me into Your family!

PART OF HIS PLAN

In him we were also chosen, having been predestined according to the plan of him who works out everything in conformity with the purpose of his will, in order that we, who were the first to put our hope in Christ, might be for the praise of his glory.

Ephesians 1:11–12 NIV

Some people like to think of the big picture, while others are detail oriented. Both perspectives come with their own set of strengths, and the world definitely needs both big-picture and detail-oriented people.

It should come as no surprise that God is God, and as Creator of all, He knows both the big picture and every single detail. He has a plan for every person and everything that happens in the universe. And you are part of His plan.

The great thing is that God keeps working absolutely every single detail to go along with His purpose and plan. He's never surprised. He never wonders what will happen next. He knows because He has the power and might to plan it all.

Lord God, I may not know what's happening in my future, but You do! I'm really thankful I can trust in Your plan.

HAPPILY EVER AFTER

Then I saw a new heaven and a new earth, for the first heaven and the first earth had passed away, and the sea was no more. And I saw the holy city, new Jerusalem, coming down out of heaven from God, prepared as a bride adorned for her husband. And I heard a loud voice from the throne saying, "Behold, the dwelling place of God is with man. He will dwell with them, and they will be his people, and God himself will be with them as their God."

Revelation 21:1–3 ESV

As much as you feel like you belong here on earth, this world won't last forever. In fact, the Bible tells us that this earth will be replaced with a new heaven and a new earth.

In this new home, you won't be separated from God anymore. That's spending eternity with the King of kings and Lord of lords. That's spending the rest of time in a new place with the Creator of all. That's a forever relationship with the Maker of heaven and earth.

Getting to dwell with God will be the best part. You don't have to worry about what will happen in the future, because you know the ending to your story—and you'll live happily ever after!

Father, thanks for including me as part of Your perfect forever plan!

SEEN AND HEARD

The eyes of the L*ORD* *are on the righteous,*
and his ears are attentive to their cry.
PSALM 34:15 NIV

So many times, it seems like people look past you or seem too busy to notice you're there. This feeling of invisibility can bring a flood of emotions that leave you feeling lonely and unimportant.

But God sees you. In fact, He sees every bit of what's going on in your life. He hears you too, including every word you say and every thought you think. Not a single bit of what you experience escapes His notice. He understands what you're going through because He made you.

As you begin to realize that God is right there paying attention to you with great love and care, don't be afraid to talk to Him. Open up with all your thoughts and feelings, both good and bad. Pour out your heart to Him, knowing that He does listen. His eyes are on you, and you can find comfort and help through Him.

Lord, thank You for seeing me! Thank You for hearing me! Thank You for knowing me completely and choosing to love me anyway.

THE BEST HELPER

"I will ask the Father, and he will give you another Helper, to be with you forever, even the Spirit of truth, whom the world cannot receive, because it neither sees him nor knows him. You know him, for he dwells with you and will be in you."

John 14:16–17 ESV

After Jesus was crucified, dead, and resurrected, He knew He wasn't leaving His faithful followers alone. It might have seemed like He wouldn't be with them anymore, but when He ascended to heaven, His believers were filled with the Holy Spirit.

The Holy Spirit, or the Spirit of truth, becomes part of believers of Christ. He moves in as an assurance that you're now the Lord's. Being filled with the Spirit comes only when you believe in Christ. It's nothing the unbelieving world will experience.

Once the Holy Spirit is living inside you, you'll begin to notice the amazing ways He leads and guides you. This Spirit will be with you forever, leading and guiding you as you listen to Him and honor Him.

Father, thank You so much for the gift of Your Holy Spirit! I'm glad He'll never leave me. I'm glad He'll be with me forever!

BEAUTIFUL!

God has made everything beautiful for its own time. He has planted eternity in the human heart, but even so, people cannot see the whole scope of God's work from beginning to end.

Ecclesiastes 3:11 NLT

Could something that's ugly be considered beautiful? Of course it could! God has a way of working things out so even if they seem hideous, they'll eventually become beautiful.

Beauty, though, so often seems hidden. You might struggle to find any hint of beauty when something appears to be horrid. Yet God is working behind the scenes, transforming even the ugliest parts of this world into something beautiful that will bring Him honor and glory.

Sometimes you might see the transformation with your own eyes, and you'll be surprised at the miracles God has performed. But other times you'll just have to trust that He's in the middle of bringing beauty into the most hideous spaces. As the master artist, though, He has a method behind His masterpiece. And when He's finished, it will be astonishingly beautiful!

Lord, I'm amazed that You will make absolutely everything beautiful for its own time. I'm excited to watch Your work and to spy Your progress!

RAISED UP

"For this purpose I have raised you up, to show you my power, so that my name may be proclaimed in all the earth."

Exodus 9:16 ESV

When you consider yourself and how you're just a normal girl, it can be pretty astonishing to realize that God can show you His power in amazing ways. He can even use you to be part of His plan!

God used a normal man like Moses to confront Pharaoh and to bring some amazing wonders to the Egyptians. Moses didn't have any power on his own, but the Lord worked powerfully through him.

Similarly, you don't have any power on your own either. But God can work through you. And if you're willing to be used by Him, He can work through you in pretty amazing ways!

How can you begin this process? Simply ask Him! Thank Him for His power, then ask Him to use you in a mighty way for His glory. Get ready to watch the way He'll work!

Father, thank You for showing Your power through ordinary people. Please use me and my life to glorify You!

THE PERFECT GIFT

Whatever is good and perfect is a gift coming down to us from God our Father, who created all the lights in the heavens. He never changes or casts a shifting shadow. He chose to give birth to us by giving us his true word. And we, out of all creation, became his prized possession.

James 1:17–18 NLT

Really thoughtful gifts are such a treat to receive! Not much can compare to realizing the gift giver has thought about exactly what you want or need and then surprised you with a perfect gift.

God gives good gifts too. He is filled with love and generosity, and He pours out His thoughtful care to you with His perfect gifts. He might surprise you with something you've always hoped for or dreamed about, or He might give you something really wonderful that you never even imagined. Because you're His prized possession, He delights in you! He shows some of that delight in the way He fills your life with wonderful things you could never buy or earn on your own.

Father, thank You for Your wonderful gifts! I'm thankful for the way You surprise me so perfectly!

ENEMIES TO FRIENDS

Once you were alienated from God and were enemies in your minds because of your evil behavior. But now he has reconciled you by Christ's physical body through death to present you holy in his sight, without blemish and free from accusation—if you continue in your faith, established and firm, and do not move from the hope held out in the gospel.

Colossians 1:21–23 NIV

When people oppose you, it's easy to hold a grudge and consider them as enemies. Before you knew Jesus, you were alienated from God. Your sins proved you were like His enemy.

But Jesus changed everything. Once you stepped out in faith and accepted Him as your Lord, He alone made you right with God. Now you're seen as holy instead of evil. You belong instead of being an outsider.

Keep strengthening your faith until it's as solid as a rock, and keep your hope in Jesus. As you do, you'll be God's friend. His daughter. You won't be His enemy anymore.

Jesus, thank You for changing my relationship with the Father! Through You I'm accepted. I'm now a friend of God.

MY FOREVER HOME

But we are citizens of heaven, where the Lord Jesus Christ lives. And we are eagerly waiting for him to return as our Savior. He will take our weak mortal bodies and change them into glorious bodies like his own, using the same power with which he will bring everything under his control.

PHILIPPIANS 3:20–21 NLT

It can be tough to realize that tomorrow is never guaranteed. And it's just as tough to remember that this world isn't your forever home. But it's not.

As long as you choose to trust in Christ, you have a future with Him in heaven. You will belong there with Him, where you'll actually get to see Him. Once you're there, He'll change you. You'll have a glorious, immortal body that won't be weak or frail. Your body won't get hurt, and you won't have to think about getting old or dying. Nothing will seem out of place or chaotic or stressful anymore. Instead, everything will be brought under His control. That's a place worth staying in forever!

Lord Jesus, I'm glad You'll return someday. I'm glad You'll change my body into something glorious and eternal. And I'm glad I'll get to worship You face-to-face.

NO MORE FEAR!

"So do not fear, for I am with you; do not be dismayed, for I am your God. I will strengthen you and help you; I will uphold you with my righteous right hand."

Isaiah 41:10 NIV

What are you afraid of? When you think of fears and phobias, what scares you?

No matter what sends shivers up your spine, know that the Lord can free you from fear. That's right! Through Jesus you don't have to fear. You don't have to be dismayed. You don't have to worry.

How can you be free from fear through the Lord? When you have a relationship with Him, He is with you. His Holy Spirit fills you and helps you. He strengthens you in an amazing way. And your fear? It vanishes in His presence. His strength and peace flood you like nothing else, and you can live a life of courage and strength.

Father, thank You for Your strength! Thank You for Your courage! It is such a huge relief to know that, through You, I don't have to fear anymore!

SEEN

Thereafter, Hagar used another name to refer to the Lord, who had spoken to her. She said, "You are the God who sees me."

Genesis 16:13 NLT

It can be easy to feel invisible, like no one notices you or like everyone forgets about you and your opinion. You can feel overlooked and passed up, even when you try to speak up.

But God? He notices you. In fact, He's the God who sees you! He sees what you're going through. He hears your prayers. He knows when you're having a good day and when your day is one of the worst you've had. He's always there, always seeing, always knowing.

The next time you feel alone and forgotten, tell the Lord about it. Honestly pour out all your feelings to Him. Not only will you be seen, but you'll also be heard.

Father God, I am so glad You are the God who sees me. Thanks for never leaving me alone. Thank You for caring about me and what I'm facing.

JUST LIKE JESUS

Therefore be imitators of God, as beloved children. And walk in love, as Christ loved us and gave himself up for us, a fragrant offering and sacrifice to God.

Ephesians 5:1–2 esv

If you're trying to imitate someone, you carefully pay attention to what that person says or does. If you're trying to repeat someone word for word, you listen closely. If you want to copy someone's mannerisms, you notice tiny details. And if you want to become more like someone else, you focus on what that person does, whether it's what they wear or how they treat others.

As a deeply loved child of God, a way to show your love is to try to imitate Jesus. He lived a perfect life, and even though you'll never be perfect in this life, it's still a great goal to follow Him. He's the one to copy. He's worth imitating. Just as His life was filled with love for others, a great way to follow Him is to be filled with love for others too.

Lord Jesus, I want to be like You. Please help me love others like You love. Please help me give of myself for others too, just like You did.

FILLED WITH HIS LOVE

"I have loved you even as the Father has loved me. Remain in my love. When you obey my commandments, you remain in my love, just as I obey my Father's commandments and remain in his love."

JOHN 15:9–10 NLT

Everyone wants to be loved. But while you can spend a lot of time wishing and hoping for love, it's not always easy to find. Other people may not share your same feelings—either they love you less or more than you'd prefer.

But the love God has for you? It fills the emptiness you feel. The love Jesus poured out for you is immense. It's the one thing that actually can satisfy your need for love.

Once you're filled with His love, you can start sharing it with others. You can continue to remain in His love. It won't disappear and leave you alone. That kind of love from Jesus can't be faked or bought or forced. It's the real deal. And it's amazing.

Lord Jesus, thank You for loving me like the Father has loved You. I want to stay in Your love forever!

WHATEVER YOU DO

Commit to the Lord whatever you do,
and he will establish your plans.

Proverbs 16:3 NIV

Hoping and dreaming about your future can be fun. It's easy to fantasize about anything—from who you might marry to what kind of job you'll have to the amazing places you'll see.

Sometimes you can even use those dreams to help you make goals and plans for your life. But as much as you plan out your future, keep a few things in mind.

First of all, plans aren't certain. Just because you'd like to prepare for something doesn't mean it will become a reality. Second, you can plan all you'd like, but the Lord is the one who establishes your plans.

As you remember that God is the one in control and commit to Him all the things you're doing and would like to do, He'll guide your dreams and plans. He might even make them a reality!

Lord, You know my heart. You know my deepest hopes and my greatest dreams. I pray that I'll listen to Your leading. I want to honor You with what I do. Please establish my plans!

FREEDOM!

So now there is no condemnation for those who belong to Christ Jesus. And because you belong to him, the power of the life-giving Spirit has freed you from the power of sin that leads to death.

Romans 8:1–2 NLT

Look around and you'll spot condemnation everywhere. Are you different from other people? You might face judgment. Do you disagree with someone else's opinion? You might get ridiculed. Have you stood up for your beliefs? You might feel like an outsider.

The thing is, when you belong to Jesus, you won't face condemnation. Instead, you'll experience His acceptance. You don't have to feel like a prisoner tied to the vicious, unforgiving feeling of your sins and the consequences that come as a result of those sins. Because of Jesus, you're truly free. No more judgment. No more ridicule. No more life on the outside. Because of Jesus, you don't have to worry about facing eternal condemnation.

Lord Jesus, Your freedom is an amazing gift! Thank You for rescuing me from the cycle of sin, condemnation, and death. Thank You for the true freedom that comes only from You!

PART OF HIS PLAN

Lord, you are my God; I will exalt you and praise your name, for in perfect faithfulness you have done wonderful things, things planned long ago.

Isaiah 25:1 NIV

Planning ahead can be a really helpful habit. You can plan when you'll work on school projects so you don't have to rush to finish all the work at the last minute, or think ahead as to what you'll need to do in the next season or next year.

But even your best plans aren't guaranteed. Circumstances can change in the blink of an eye and your plans can seem ruined.

God's plans are different. He made plans for your life long, long ago, and He's working them out even right now. He's faithfully in the middle of doing wonderful things for you and with you. Even if things don't seem to be perfect right now, you can trust Him and His very good plans. And you can praise Him for the wonderful things He's doing in your life!

Father, it's pretty amazing to consider that You've made plans for me. I can hardly wait to see what they are!

TEARS IN A BOTTLE

You keep track of all my sorrows. You have collected all my tears in your bottle. You have recorded each one in your book.

Psalm 56:8 NLT

When you have a really bad day, it's easy to feel like no one cares about you or your feelings. It's easy to feel like you're all alone.

But you're not alone. In fact, God pays attention to every tiny detail of you and your life. He keeps track of all of your sorrows. He pays attention to what brings you joy too! He collects all your tears. He knows what breaks your heart, and He knows exactly why you're crying.

In all of your disappointment and sadness, the Lord sees you. He hears you. He knows your heart. And if He could wrap His arms around you to hold you tight as you cry, He would. He loves you. He wants the best for you. And He is there for you, always listening to your prayers and always waiting for you to bring your worries and heartbreaks to Him.

Father God, thank You for not just noticing me but for caring so very much for me.

WAITING FOR SOMETHING BETTER

But as it is, they desire a better country, that is, a heavenly one. Therefore God is not ashamed to be called their God, for he has prepared for them a city.

Hebrews 11:16 ESV

Ever feel like you don't completely fit in with this world? Or even like you don't fit in with your friends or family?

It's totally normal to wonder if you belong. And it's normal to feel awkward or wonder who you're supposed to be or what you're supposed to do.

The thing is, you're here on this earth only for a little while. You're passing through on your way to your permanent home. God has prepared this better, forever home for you, and you'll fit into it just perfectly.

You can make the most of your time here without getting too attached to things of this world. You might even want to remember you're here on a journey. Then, every time you feel out of place, remind yourself that this world isn't your home.

Father, when I feel out of place here, please help me remember it's because I'm waiting for my forever home. I don't have to fit in right now!

ALWAYS HAVE HOPE

As for me, I will always have hope; I will praise you more and more. My mouth will tell of your righteous deeds, of your saving acts all day long—though I know not how to relate them all.

Psalm 71:14–15 NIV

Have you ever considered what it would be like to have hope that never ever runs out?

There's only one way to have never-ending hope, and that's through the Lord. He has authored your faith and will perfect it. He's working out His perfect plan, and He has an absolutely amazing eternity in heaven ready and waiting.

To know that God knows and works in every single detail is mind-blowing. Even on your darkest days, in your most questionable circumstances, He's worthy of your praise. And He's worthy of your hope.

When you're filled with God's hope and see the way He's doing amazing things in your life or in the world around you, be sure to thank Him, and then tell someone else about what He has done!

Father, I'm so glad I can hope in You! I praise You for all Your righteous deeds and the way You work in my life.

A GOOD PLAN

"For I know the plans I have for you,"
says the Lord. "They are plans for good and not
for disaster, to give you a future and a hope."

Jeremiah 29:11 NLT

The Lord has had good plans for His chosen people, the Israelites, since the Old Testament. Once you trust and believe in Jesus, you're forgiven and accepted into God's family. Now that you're a daughter of God, He looks at you with favor, just as He does His chosen people.

Because you've been adopted into God's family, He looks at you with favor and plans good things for your life. In fact, you can anticipate the future with great hope because of all the amazing plans He has for you.

Even if and when it seems like nothing is working out, or if the plans you've had for yourself seem ruined, you don't have to fear. Trust that the Lord is doing something truly wonderful. Even if it doesn't feel like it now, His plans are for good. He just might surprise you with how wonderful they are!

Lord, it's a relief to know that You already have plans for my future and that they're really good. I'm thankful I can put my total trust in You!

EASING A BROKEN HEART

The LORD is close to the brokenhearted;
he rescues those whose spirits are crushed.
PSALM 34:18 NLT

Some people are repelled by pain and hurry to get away from someone who cries or is feeling down. But other people gravitate toward the lonely and brokenhearted. With great kindness, they listen quietly and ask caring questions. They don't make the sad person feel worse for needing to cry. They don't scold them over tears or pain. They just listen with sympathy.

Even better than a wonderful and truly caring, sympathetic person on earth, the Lord is the ultimate listener and comforter. He's always close to the brokenhearted. And while sad situations may remain sad for a while, God steps in to comfort people who need it. He rescues people who suffer. This kind of rescue might look like a change of circumstances, kindness shared by other people, or unspoken comfort. But God does rescue in amazing ways. Like a breath of fresh air, He enters our lowest, hardest situations and adds comfort and peace.

Lord, it's so comforting to know You're close to the brokenhearted. And You're a rescuer! Please rescue me just when I need You.

A FATHER'S LOVE

"My son, do not regard lightly the discipline of the Lord, nor be weary when reproved by him. For the Lord disciplines the one he loves, and chastises every son whom he receives." It is for discipline that you have to endure. God is treating you as sons. For what son is there whom his father does not discipline?

HEBREWS 12:5–7 ESV

Not many people appreciate discipline. Whether you're trying to add discipline to your life or you're corrected by an authority figure, it can feel really uncomfortable. Similarly, it's not enjoyable to endure the Lord's discipline.

Yet the Lord's discipline should be what you welcome the most. God chooses to discipline you because you're His daughter and He loves you. If He didn't love you so much, He'd let you go along your own way, without correcting or shaping you into the young woman He'd like you to become.

Even when discipline feels uncomfortable, it's a really good thing because it helps make you become more like Christ.

Lord, I may not like to admit this, but thank You for Your discipline. Thank You for valuing and loving me so much that You correct me for my own good.

SURROUNDED BY HIS PROTECTION

"Don't be afraid!" Elisha told [his servant]. "For there are more on our side than on theirs!" Then Elisha prayed, "O Lord, open his eyes and let him see!" The Lord opened the young man's eyes, and when he looked up, he saw that the hillside around Elisha was filled with horses and chariots of fire.

2 Kings 6:16–17 NLT

The Bible is filled with extraordinary stories of how God protected and worked for the Israelites in amazing ways. One of those examples was with the prophet Elisha. Elisha always knew when the enemy was planning to attack. Frustrated, his adversaries came at night and surrounded the city where Elisha was staying. When Elisha's servant saw the enemy troops, he panicked.

Elisha, however, had no fear. Instead, he knew he was surrounded by the Lord's protection. And Elisha's enemies never did attack.

Just as the Lord protected Elisha in a spectacular way, He'll protect you too. You may not be able to see it, but He's protecting you in miraculous ways!

Father, thank You for all of the ways You protect me! I'll never know exactly what You do or how You do it, but I'm really glad You do!

A PURPOSE FOR EVERYTHING

The Lord has made everything for its purpose,
even the wicked for the day of trouble.
Proverbs 16:4 esv

Some days life seems really random. It's hard to understand why certain things happen and almost impossible to connect the dots and figure out how different events could be related to one another.

The great thing with God, though, is that nothing is random. Nothing! He makes everything for a purpose, and He works every single detail together as part of His plan. He doesn't stick to only the good things. He uses bad things too. He even uses the wicked in different ways.

Instead of getting upset when it seems like the wicked are triumphing or really awful things are happening, relax and remember that God has a reason for all of it. Just because you don't understand what's going on doesn't mean He doesn't understand!

Lord, it's amazing that You've made absolutely everything for a purpose—even things or people that seem pretty awful. Please help me trust You and wait while You work out Your perfect plan!

UNTHINKABLE KINDNESS

God showed his great love for us by sending Christ to die for us while we were still sinners. And since we have been made right in God's sight by the blood of Christ, he will certainly save us from God's condemnation. For since our friendship with God was restored by the death of his Son while we were still his enemies, we will certainly be saved through the life of his Son.

ROMANS 5:8–10 NLT

Have you ever gone out of your way to do something nice for someone else? What did you do? How much of a sacrifice did you make?

As kind or generous as you were, God gave a bigger sacrifice—His only Son. It's not like anyone deserves His gift. In fact, He chose to make that sacrifice when you were considered His enemy.

It's pretty remarkable to be kind to someone who has wronged you. But to give your most prized treasure to your enemy? What unthinkable kindness! That generosity and selflessness is unlike anything you've ever seen. And it all was made for you.

Lord, I don't deserve Jesus' sacrifice. But I'm thankful for it!

TURNING HEAD KNOWLEDGE INTO HEART KNOWLEDGE

May the Lord lead your hearts into a full understanding and expression of the love of God and the patient endurance that comes from Christ.

2 Thessalonians 3:5 NLT

Have you ever heard about the difference between head knowledge and heart knowledge? Head knowledge involves knowing something in your mind; you understand the information, concepts, or logic. Heart knowledge is different. It means you process the information so it affects your heart. It changes the way you feel and what you believe.

You may hear about the love of God and feel like you understand it. You've learned about it and have heard that God is love. But has His love actually changed your heart? Do you feel different because of His love?

The Lord can lead your heart into that understanding. He can help you experience Christ's patient endurance and His love that's beyond comparison. Begin praying for Him to change your head knowledge into heart knowledge. Then get ready to experience Christ's love in a whole new way!

Father, please help me understand Your love and Your grace both with my head and my heart. I want to know You fully!

MULTIPLICATION

You have multiplied, O Lord my God, your wondrous deeds and your thoughts toward us; none can compare with you! I will proclaim and tell of them, yet they are more than can be told.

Psalm 40:5 ESV

If you think of learning about arithmetic, you could increase numbers through addition, but multiplication is a more effective and quicker way to grow. In your everyday life, you'll accomplish much more if you multiply your effort than if you simply add to it.

In Psalm 40 the psalmist tells that the Lord has multiplied His wondrous deeds and thoughts toward us. God doesn't just add a kind sentiment or a thoughtful act to your life. He multiplies beyond what you could expect or imagine.

When you notice the way God multiplies wonderful things in your life, whether they're His thoughts or His deeds, tell others about what He has done for you! Don't keep His good gifts a secret. Make sure to boast in the Lord and praise Him for His goodness and generosity.

O Lord my God, thank You for multiplying Your wondrous deeds and Your thoughts toward me! Nothing in this world can compare with You.

GUARANTEED

He who has prepared us for this very thing is God, who has given us the Spirit as a guarantee.

2 Corinthians 5:5 ESV

Sometimes in life, promises seem too good to be true. And sadly, promises sometimes *are* too good to be true and end up being broken. But God is a promise keeper. He has made some pretty amazing promises, and He has kept every single one.

One promise He has made is that He has created an eternal house in heaven. While you're here on earth, you groan and long for that eternal house. Until your moving day, God gives His Holy Spirit as a guarantee. It's like His Spirit is a down payment on your future home, holding your place there.

The Holy Spirit is your valuable guarantee while God the Father is working out what He has promised to do for you. Until you see the way He keeps His promise, you get the good gift of His Spirit!

Father, thank You for preparing a heavenly home for me so I can spend forever with You. Thanks also that You've given me Your Spirit as a guarantee. That's an amazingly good gift!

PROMISE KEEPER

"Know therefore that the Lord your God is God, the faithful God who keeps covenant and steadfast love with those who love him and keep his commandments, to a thousand generations."

Deuteronomy 7:9 ESV

In the Old Testament, the Lord worked in mighty ways in the lives of the Israelites. He made and kept amazing promises. Some of His promises apply to followers of Christ too.

As the Lord looks at a person's heart, He knows who is a true believer. He knows who trusts Him and obeys Him. He knows who loves Him deeply.

As you know that the Lord is God and you choose to love Him and keep His commandments, He passes His love on to you too. Choose to live differently than the world out of your love for Him. When you do, He'll be faithful to keep His promises. And His love and favor for you will be beautiful!

Father God, I do believe that You are my Lord. I love You! I want to obey You, even when it's difficult. Thank You for creating me to have a relationship with You. Thank You for faithfully loving me.

GIVE HIM YOUR TROUBLES

Cast all your anxiety on him because he cares for you.

1 PETER 5:7 NIV

Every single day, you have a lot to think about. Sometimes when you're really overwhelmed or in the middle of a tough situation, it's easy to focus on all that could go wrong.

Instead of dwelling on the worst, though, you don't have to keep everything bottled up inside. The Lord loves to hear what's troubling you. In fact, He invites you to give Him all your worries and cares. He would love for you to tell Him about what's bothering you then to surrender it all to Him. Every concern. Every fear. Every bit of anxiety.

Why would God want to take all the awful thoughts and feelings you're experiencing? Because He cares for you! Plus, He can set you free from all your concerns.

Even if you're not sure about sharing all of your problems or burdens with Him, try it. The freedom and peace He'll give you in return will be worth it!

Lord, being able to cast all my cares on You is so freeing. Thank You for caring for me so much that You're happy when I surrender all my anxiety to You!

HOW MANY?

"Lord, remind me how brief my time on earth will be. Remind me that my days are numbered—how fleeting my life is. . . ." We are merely moving shadows, and all our busy rushing ends in nothing. We heap up wealth, not knowing who will spend it. And so, Lord, where do I put my hope? My only hope is in you.

Psalm 39:4, 6–7 NLT

Sometimes it feels like time drags on and on, but your time here on earth actually is pretty short. In the big scheme of forever, your days go by so quickly. You're really more like a moving shadow. If you spend your time focusing on making more money or getting more belongings or accomplishing a lot, remember that the things that seem so important right now will vanish.

So what's the point? If life here on earth is quick, how should you live? You can remember how quickly your life will pass by, then hope in the Lord. Your only hope is in Him—hope for living out your days here on earth well and hope for your eternity spent with Him.

Lord, my hope is in You! Please show me how to live for You all the days of my life.

EVERY BLESSING

Blessed be the God and Father of our Lord Jesus Christ, who has blessed us in Christ with every spiritual blessing in the heavenly places, even as he chose us in him before the foundation of the world, that we should be holy and blameless before him.

Ephesians 1:3–4 ESV

From #blessed to reminders like "Count your blessings," it's easy to talk about blessings without considering what they are.

Ephesians 1 includes a lot of details about blessings, like the way God lavished you with every spiritual blessing in the heavenly places. Wait a second. *Every* spiritual blessing? That's amazing!

The Lord has heaped on every spiritual blessing just as He chose you in Him before the world was made. It's an absolute mystery to wrap your brain around the fact that long before you chose God, He chose you. Will you ever understand how or why He did this? No. But the main thing to remember is that He did it so you can be holy and blameless before Him. You can realize it's a mystery and thank Him for it!

Father, thank You for blessing me in Christ with every spiritual blessing!

A RESCUE

Have mercy on me, O God, have mercy! I look to you for protection. I will hide beneath the shadow of your wings until the danger passes by. I cry out to God Most High, to God who will fulfill his purpose for me. He will send help from heaven to rescue me, disgracing those who hound me. My God will send forth his unfailing love and faithfulness.

Psalm 57:1–3 NLT

Some days feel like bad days. And some days feel like really bad days in the terrible, horrible, no good, very bad day way.

On your worst days, you don't have to keep everything to yourself. You can run to God for protection and cry out for mercy. You can get close to Him and hide yourself in Him.

When you run and call to God, He'll help you. You'll experience His faithful love in a new way as He rescues you. As you tell Him all that's on your heart and mind, you can trust that no matter how horrible your day, God will fulfill His promise and plan for you.

Father, have mercy on me! Thank You for Your protection and rescue. I trust and love You!

THE GLOW OF DAWN

"You will tell his people how to find salvation through forgiveness of their sins. Because of God's tender mercy, the morning light from heaven is about to break upon us, to give light to those who sit in darkness and in the shadow of death, and to guide us to the path of peace."

Luke 1:77–79 NLT

Have you ever gotten up to watch the sun rise? If so, you know how the sky is so very dark with the dark of night then starts to lighten and brighten before dawn. All of a sudden, with the sky glowing beautifully, you know you'll see the sun at any moment.

Just as you're so certain the sun will appear at any moment, people waited thousands of years for the Messiah to appear. When He did, it was like heaven's dawn breaking. The people who were in darkness saw a great light: Jesus!

Because of God's mercy, He sent Jesus to this world to guide people to the path of peace. Jesus brought the most brilliant, never-ending light to all the darkness of the world.

Jesus, it's so wonderful that You came to this world. Thank You for Your gift of salvation!

WHICH PATH?

Trust in the Lord with all your heart;
do not depend on your own understanding.
Seek his will in all you do, and he will
show you which path to take.

Proverbs 3:5–6 NLT

Decisions can be so difficult, from choosing what outfit you'd like to wear to picking just one flavor of ice cream. When decisions are even bigger than clothing or food, it can be scary and overwhelming to choose just one thing that eliminates all other possibilities.

Fortunately, the Bible can help your decision-making process. As Proverbs 3:6 points out, the Lord will show you which path to take. He'll point you to the best choice.

But how can God direct your way? Start out by trusting Him completely. Stop trying to figure things out on your own. Turn to the Lord in everything you do, and He'll straighten out your decisions and lead you on the right path.

Father, I'm really thankful You'll lead me when I try to follow You. When I get scared to leave decisions in Your hand, I pray that You'll fill me with courage to obey and follow You.

HIS VERY OWN POSSESSION

The grace of God has appeared that offers salvation to all people. It teaches us to say "No" to ungodliness and worldly passions, and to live self-controlled, upright and godly lives in this present age, while we wait for the blessed hope—the appearing of the glory of our great God and Savior, Jesus Christ, who gave himself for us to redeem us from all wickedness and to purify for himself a people that are his very own, eager to do what is good.

Titus 2:11–14 NIV

When you decide to believe in Jesus, you become part of His family. You belong to Him. You don't have to worry about whether you fit into this world. Jesus lived and died as a perfect sacrifice so you wouldn't live as a captive to ungodliness or worldly desires. You could be freed from wickedness and forgiven.

Through God's power, every time you choose to do what's right in His eyes, you show yourself and people around you that you're His.

Father, thank You for rescuing me. I hope in You and pray that You'll purify me so I can live a right life for You!

BETTER THAN LIFE

Because your steadfast love is better than life, my lips will praise you.

Psalm 63:3 ESV

One of the easiest Bible verses to remember is part of 1 John 4:16: "God is love."

God is love, and the Bible says that His love is better than life. But what about His love is better than life?

His steadfast love is what's so special. But what does *steadfast* mean? It means to be fixed firmly in place. Something that's steadfast can't be moved. It's constantly loyal. It's faithful and unchanging.

You are loved by God with a love that will never move or change. His love for you is faithfully and firmly fixed in place. His love doesn't depend on what He's feeling or what you're feeling. It's dependable. It's better than life.

Because you're so completely loved by God with a love that will never change, the right response is to praise Him! Praise Him for His goodness and His amazing love. Thank Him for choosing to love you. And tell someone else about it!

Father, I praise You! Your steadfast love is better than life, and I'm completely thrilled that I get to experience it.

MY ROCK

"I lay a stone in Zion, a tested stone, a precious cornerstone for a sure foundation; the one who relies on it will never be stricken with panic."

ISAIAH 28:16 NIV

All throughout the Bible, Jesus is described as a rock. He's the foundation of the church, and He can become the foundation of your life. A foundation for a building needs to be strong. If it's a cracked or crumbling foundation, the entire building will collapse into a heap of rubble.

Jesus, as a foundation, is rock solid. He's tested and tried. He's firmly placed and prized. He's a rare, valuable gem. And if you choose to build your life on Him, you'll never be shaken. You won't be disturbed. The building of your life won't crumble and fall.

Instead, with a life built on the rock of Jesus, you'll remain standing strongly, even when you face the storms of life. Like strong, ancient buildings that still stand today, you'll remain even when it seems like everything else around you collapses.

Lord Jesus, I'm so thankful You're a strong foundation! When I build my life on You and obey Your Word, I don't have to fear.

IN HIS SHADOW

Because you are my help, I sing in the shadow of your wings.

Psalm 63:7 NIV

Think about shadows for a minute. Shadows provide cooling shade in the blazing heat of the day. They are silhouettes of objects that block light; they're not the objects themselves. You need to be fairly close to whatever object is creating the shadow to see the shadow. If you're standing outside on a sunny day, your own shadow looks like it could be connected to you.

When you choose to live close to the Lord by following Him in obedience, He will help you. In fact, you can be kept safe in the shadow of His wings.

Just like a bird keeps its babies safe under its wings, God will do the same for you! He'll hide you there and keep you safe. And under the shadow of His wings, you can sing for joy.

Even when life starts to feel overwhelming, you can take comfort in God's protection because you belong to Him.

Father, thank You for helping me! Because You love me with an everlasting love, I pray I'll take comfort in the shadow of Your wings.

OLD TO NEW

Throw off your old sinful nature and your former way of life, which is corrupted by lust and deception. Instead, let the Spirit renew your thoughts and attitudes. Put on your new nature, created to be like God—truly righteous and holy.

EPHESIANS 4:22–24 NLT

Everyone has a life before Christ. Even if you're introduced to Jesus when you're young, you still have a life before and after you give your life to Christ. Other people live long lives and never come to know Him. They might hear about Him but never commit their lives to Him.

If you choose to believe in Christ and want to follow Him, tell Him right now. Not only will you be forgiven for all the ways you've sinned in the past, but the Holy Spirit—God Himself!—also will come to live in you. You'll be a new person as He guides and directs you. Instead of fear and frustration, you'll start living a life of peace and purpose.

When you have a new life in Christ, you can get rid of your old way of living and trade it for a much better life.

Father, it's amazing that You offer me a new, better life through Jesus. I'm so glad I don't have to stay trapped in my old way of living! You choose me, and I accept Your invitation to come into Your family!

CLING-WORTHY

My soul clings to you; your right hand upholds me.

Psalm 63:8 ESV

When you were young, do you remember clinging to someone you trusted? Maybe it was your mom or dad, or maybe a grandparent or older sibling. Whoever it might have been, think about what it felt like to cling to them. You didn't want to let go, right? With all of your strength, you wrapped your body around them in such a way to hold on tight.

Now that you're older, you may not cling to many people for love or protection. But you can use that same clinging action to hold on to the Lord. Just like when you were young and clingy, your soul can wrap around God and hang on tight.

Why would you want to be stuck so tightly to God that you'd need to be pried off? For starters, He loves you totally and completely. He wants what's best for you. And He holds you up every day of your life. He supports you, raises you up, and keeps you from falling. If anyone is cling-worthy, it's the Lord!

Father, I want to cling to You! I trust You completely, and I'm thankful for Your love.

A LIFE OF FREEDOM

For you have been called to live in freedom, my brothers and sisters. But don't use your freedom to satisfy your sinful nature. Instead, use your freedom to serve one another in love. For the whole law can be summed up in this one command: "Love your neighbor as yourself." But if you are always biting and devouring one another, watch out! Beware of destroying one another.

GALATIANS 5:13–15 NLT

Apart from Christ, you're a slave to sin and death. You can't help that you're shackled to your sinful way of life. But in Christ? You have freedom! You're free from the bondage of your sins.

If and when you commit your life to Christ, don't use His freedom to keep sinning just to experience more and more forgiveness. Instead, use your freedom to live a life of love! Step out in faith to love the unlovable of this world. Help other people. Loving others with kindness and thoughtfulness and mercy is a fantastic way to show your freedom in Christ.

Lord Jesus, You lived a life of love when You were here on earth. I want to be just like You! Please help me use my freedom in You to love others well.

HIS PEOPLE

Know that the Lord is God. It is he who made us, and we are his; we are his people, the sheep of his pasture.

Psalm 100:3 NIV

Think of a time when you felt left out of something. It hurt, didn't it? It's never any fun to feel excluded or like you're not part of a group.

The great news is that in the Lord's eyes, once you believe in Him, you're part of His group. You're included in His favorites. He hasn't excluded you.

How did you become part of God's people? This wasn't something you were naturally born into, and it wasn't anything you earned by good things you did. He chose you. He wanted you to be part of His family. But to be part of His family, you reached a point where you recognized Him as Lord and committed your life to Him.

Now that you're part of God's family, enjoy it! You're His people. He made you, and you are His. Thank Him for being a loving Father who chose to include you in His family!

Father God, thank You for including me in Your family. I'm so grateful to be Your child.

LIFTED UP AND CARRIED

In all their distress he too was distressed, and the angel of his presence saved them. In his love and mercy he redeemed them; he lifted them up and carried them all the days of old.

Isaiah 63:9 NIV

If you've spent all day walking or working hard, your body will feel very tired. Sometimes you can actually feel so tired and worn out that you wish someone would pick you up and carry you. This can happen if your physical strength is spent, but it can happen emotionally too. Maybe you've faced trial after trial and you just don't feel like you can handle one more thing.

The amazing news is that you can collapse into the arms of your loving heavenly Father. He will lift you up when you're weak. He can and will carry you. He knows when you're going through troubles, and because He loves you, He'll make things right through His mercy.

Father, what a relief that You're for me! In Your love and mercy, You'll help me through my toughest situations. You'll even lift me up and carry me when I need You the most.

BIGGER PLANS

Now may the God of peace who brought again from the dead our Lord Jesus, the great shepherd of the sheep, by the blood of the eternal covenant, equip you with everything good that you may do his will, working in us that which is pleasing in his sight, through Jesus Christ.

Hebrews 13:20–21 ESV

God is a God of miracles. Not just miracles like multiplying food or healing the sick, but raising Jesus back to life after He was dead for three days. He also faithfully shepherds those who believe in Him, and He has made covenants that last for eternity.

Just as God can do unthinkably huge things in this world, He also equips you in every way so you can do His will. That means He takes care of every detail and gives you everything you need to do His work. Nothing will stop Him from working in you to do what's pleasing to Him. Nothing. Through Jesus Christ, He has bigger plans for you, and He's preparing and equipping you to do those things even now.

Father, help me understand Your plans for me. Please help me trust You completely as You prepare and equip me for Your good work!

WHAT'S THE PLAN?

In their hearts humans plan their course,
but the Lord establishes their steps.
Proverbs 16:9 NIV

You know what you'd like to do. You know when you'd love to do it. Depending on how much you like to dream, you might try to imagine every step to reach your goals.

Dreaming and hoping and planning aren't bad. In fact, setting goals is a great way to live with direction and purpose. But just because you plan how you'd like something to work out doesn't mean it will. In fact, your plans are never guaranteed. There's even a good chance they won't work out. And that's okay.

As you think about your present and your future, keep dreaming. Keep thinking about what you'd like to do with your life. But as you dream, remember that the Lord is the one who will establish your steps. He's the one who will make your plans into reality in His own timing and in His own way.

As you trust Him with your plans, He'll surprise you with a future that's better than you can ever imagine.

Father, please help me relax and trust You completely with my future! Please guide my plans too.

KNOWN

Nevertheless, God's solid foundation stands firm, sealed with this inscription: "The Lord knows those who are his," and, "Everyone who confesses the name of the Lord must turn away from wickedness."

2 Timothy 2:19 niv

Think about your treasured possessions. What are they? And why are they so special to you? Are they meaningful because of a certain memory? Did someone give you these items as a gift? Did you find something in an unusual way or at a unique location?

Just as you know your treasured possessions and what makes them so meaningful to you, the Lord knows you too. To Him you are a treasured possession. He paid a great cost for you—His Son's life—and that makes you of tremendous importance and value to Him.

As you confess the name of the Lord and turn to Him, He delights in you. He knows you are His, and He loves and adores you.

Father, it is so very good to be known by You! I confess that You are Lord. I praise You for Your goodness and thank You for Your faithfulness that never ends.

MY FORTRESS

Yes, my soul, find rest in God; my hope comes from him. Truly he is my rock and my salvation; he is my fortress, I will not be shaken.

Psalm 62:5–6 niv

If you've ever seen a castle or military fort, think about how it's surrounded by a fortress. If the gates to the fortress are closed, there's no way in. You can't climb the walls or even push your way in. A fortress creates a safe and secure place.

Just as physical fortresses defend, the Lord is your fortress. He protects you. Through Him, you're saved. With Him on your side, you won't be shaken even when enemies attack and you feel like you're in the middle of a battle.

Because the Lord is your strong and sure defense, you don't have to worry. In fact, you can rest in Him—not just relax and let down your guard, but truly rest. He's your safe place. He's your protection. He's your fortress.

Lord, thank You for being my safe place and my protection! I wouldn't want anything or anyone else to be my fortress.

STRENGTHENED AND FILLED

We also pray that you will be strengthened with all his glorious power so you will have all the endurance and patience you need. May you be filled with joy, always thanking the Father. He has enabled you to share in the inheritance that belongs to his people, who live in the light.

Colossians 1:11–12 NLT

Some activities and relationships feel so draining. As much as you invest time and energy into them, they leave you feeling zapped. Instead of feeling energized, you feel depleted and worn out.

God is not like that. In fact, He gives strength with all of His glorious power, and He fills you with joy. There's no lack of energy with Him—He fills you up so you feel alive!

As He strengthens you with His own power, you're able to use it to endure patiently. Even when you face energy-zapping situations, His power will give you strength to endure, along with a healthy dose of His joy. He'll add pep to your step.

Thank You, Lord, for Your strength! It's amazing to be filled with Your power and joy. Thank You! Sometimes I really need it to endure.

KNOWING AND UNDERSTANDING

I pray for you constantly, asking God, the glorious Father of our Lord Jesus Christ, to give you spiritual wisdom and insight so that you might grow in your knowledge of God. I pray that your hearts will be flooded with light so that you can understand the confident hope he has given to those he called—his holy people who are his rich and glorious inheritance.

Ephesians 1:16–18 NLT

When you first believe in Christ, you're made right in Him, or justified. This starts a long journey that will last the rest of your life as He helps you become more and more like Him.

The good news is that you don't have to worry about this process. You're not left alone to figure it out on your own. The Lord can and will give you wisdom and insight. As He does, you'll grow in your knowledge and understanding of Him. You may not instantly understand everything, but over time He'll help you grow more and more.

Father, I'm so relieved I don't have to figure out spiritual details on my own. Please fill me with Your wisdom and insight so I can learn more about You—and who I am in You.

EVERLASTING LOVE

From everlasting to everlasting the LORD's love is with those who fear him, and his righteousness with their children's children.

PSALM 103:17 NIV

Everlasting love sounds so dreamy, doesn't it? It's almost like something that should be the title of a romantic movie or something only written about in a novel.

But everlasting love is exactly what the Lord has for you. Simply put, His love for you will last forever. It will go on and on and on. He'll never stop loving you. In fact, He loves you so much that His love and favor for you eventually will even spill over onto your children and grandchildren.

This kind of love isn't for every person on the planet. Sadly, some people don't want God's love. And because of their choices, they won't get it. But as you fear Him and respect Him as the Lord of ords, He'll always and forever wow you with the amazing love He has for you.

Father, Your love for me is pretty amazing. I'm blown away by the fact that it will never end. Thank You! I love You too!

NO REASON

He has saved us and called us to a holy life—
not because of anything we have done but because
of his own purpose and grace. This grace was given
us in Christ Jesus before the beginning of time.

2 TIMOTHY 1:9 NIV

Have you ever been chosen for something that in some way wasn't performance based? It didn't matter what you did or didn't do, but you received some sort of favor or gift anyway.

Your relationship with Christ is like that. It doesn't matter who you are or what you've done. If He has called you to Himself, it's because He chose you for His very own purpose.

Would you like to hear the wildest part? It was His plan to choose you and heap all that favor on you before the beginning of time. He called you to a holy life and knew that one day He would save you. If that's not a fantastic reason to thank God, what else could be?

Thank You for thinking of me and saving me and having a plan for my life even before the beginning of time. I want to live for You!

PRAISE HIM!

Praise the Lord, all you nations. Praise him, all you people of the earth. For his unfailing love for us is powerful; the Lord's faithfulness endures forever. Praise the Lord!

Psalm 117 NLT

When you think about all the Lord has done for you, it seems only natural to praise Him. He's deserving of your praise. He loves you with a powerful, never-ending, never-stopping love. He's forever faithful. That's worthy of praise!

If you look to the world around you and see all that God has done and is doing, a right response is to praise Him. Does His creation take your breath away? Praise Him for His artistry and creativity! Do you stand amazed at the way He works out tiny details? Praise Him! When you think of what you deserve because of the way you have sometimes disappointed Him by your disobedience yet how He heaps blessing after blessing on you, praise Him! The Lord is great. And He's greatly to be praised.

God, I praise You for being Lord of all. I praise You for being so great yet taking notice of me. And You do so much more than take notice— You pour out Your love and favor on me. Thank You!

APPROACHING GOD'S THRONE

Let us then approach God's throne of grace with confidence, so that we may receive mercy and find grace to help us in our time of need.

Hebrews 4:16 NIV

Imagine the lavish throne of a king. Crafted from gold or marble, it might be covered in a rich velvet or priceless tapestry and embellished with gems. Just seeing that throne would help you realize you were in the presence of royalty. And if you saw a king sitting on his throne? You'd feel humbled and awkward as you tried to decide whether to bow or curtsy or fall to your knees.

If you'd approach an earthly king and his throne like this, it seems like you'd be completely humbled and terrified when approaching the throne of the King of kings. Yet the book of Hebrews says you can approach God's throne of grace with confidence. Say what? Confidence instead of trembling and dread?

When you do approach God's throne, He'll give you mercy and grace. He'll help you when you need Him the most. Instead of shaking with fear, you can come toward Him confidently, knowing that He loves you and wants to help you.

Jesus, I worship You as King of kings. Thank You for Your kindness and favor so I can approach You!

ENDURANCE

Give thanks to the LORD, for he is good; his love endures forever.

PSALM 118:1 NIV

When you think of endurance, it's easy to think of a situation or condition that's difficult or unpleasant. But God's love for you endures forever, and it's not uncomfortable for Him. In fact, His love endures in a lasting way because it's durable and can withstand anything. Anything! His love is patient. It's solid. It's not going to give in.

He's not like anyone else you know, because people aren't always good. They're not always loving. Unfortunately, you can't rely on a person's ability to endure.

Because the Lord's love is so reliable, so enduring, and because it lasts forever, it's worth thanking Him. Because the Lord is good, it's worth thanking Him too! He could be unkind or unloving, but He is goodness. He is love. And because He chooses to treat you with His goodness and love, it's only a natural response to thank Him. Instead of taking Him for granted, be grateful to be loved by Him!

Thank You, Father, for being so good to me. It's such a gift to be loved by You.

A PLACE TO BELONG

"My Father's house has many rooms;
if that were not so, would I have told you
that I am going there to prepare a place for
you? And if I go and prepare a place for you,
I will come back and take you to be with me
that you also may be where I am. You know
the way to the place where I am going."

John 14:2–4 NIV

Knowing where you'll live is a huge comfort. Being unsure about where you'll stay—even for one night—can leave you feeling insecure and stressed. Figuring out where you'll stay for an extended time brings a big sense of relief. You can settle in. Even if it's someplace new, you can make it feel like a home.

Right now Jesus is preparing a place for you to stay. He's fixing a room just for you in His Father's house—in heaven! Realizing He's preparing an eternal home for you is super comforting. You don't have to stress about what you'll do once this life is over. You'll belong with Him!

Jesus, You know me so well. It's a huge comfort to know You're preparing a place for me even right now. Thank You!

NO WORRIES!

"Therefore I tell you, do not worry about your life, what you will eat or drink; or about your body, what you will wear. Is not life more than food, and the body more than clothes? Look at the birds of the air; they do not sow or reap or store away in barns, and yet your heavenly Father feeds them. Are you not much more valuable than they? Can any one of you by worrying add a single hour to your life?"

MATTHEW 6:25–27 NIV

When was the last time you wondered about what you'd eat or what you should wear? It can seem natural to think about meals and outfits, and sometimes it's tempting to worry about them. But Jesus taught that you don't have to worry about things like food or clothing.

You don't have to worry, because you're worth much more than clothing or food. Who you are, deep down, is so much more than the things you put inside or outside your body. It's that inner you—the real you—you should consider.

The Lord knows what you need, and He'll faithfully provide for you. Forget about what's trivial and focus on what will last.

Father, thank You for providing everything I could ever need!

DEATH TO LIFE

Because of his great love for us, God, who is rich in mercy, made us alive with Christ even when we were dead in transgressions—it is by grace you have been saved.

Ephesians 2:4–5 niv

If someone you've loved has died, you already know the painful reality of death. As much as you want to see and talk to that person again—you miss so much about them!—they're not here.

Being separated from someone because of death hurts. God knows that, and it never was part of His plan. Sin brought death and separation into God's perfect world.

God hated death so much—and He loved you so very much—that He made a way to get rid of the separation of death. He sent Jesus to this world to live a perfect life, die a horrific death, rise from the dead, and live forever.

Since Jesus conquered death, everyone who trusts in Him and His resurrected life will experience the same life after death. Through His great grace, God makes you alive with Christ!

Father, I could never save myself, and I know it. But You sent Jesus so that I could be made alive after death here on earth. Thank You!

WONDERFULLY MADE

You formed my inward parts; you knitted me together in my mother's womb. I praise you, for I am fearfully and wonderfully made. Wonderful are your works; my soul knows it very well.

Psalm 139:13–14 ESV

Do you realize there's nothing accidental about you? You were formed *on* purpose *with* a purpose. God formed you—all of you. He had a plan for you and your life, and then He knit you together wonderfully.

Sometimes, if you're having a bad day, it's hard to remember that you're wonderfully made. You might not feel wonderful at all. It might seem too easy to focus on your flaws. But your feelings don't change facts.

What actually is true is that the Lord did make you in a wonderful way. He's the God of the universe and chose to make you just the way you are. When you find yourself doubting the way you've been made, ask Him to help you see yourself the way He sees you.

Father, sometimes I have a really hard time believing You made me in a wonderful way. Please help me respect what You've created. And please help me find my worth in You rather than in my forever-changing feelings.

CHANGING

And I am sure of this, that he who began a good work in you will bring it to completion at the day of Jesus Christ.

PHILIPPIANS 1:6 ESV

How patient are you with yourself? When you know you should change or improve something, do you pressure yourself to get better right away? Do you feel frustrated or annoyed that you haven't already changed?

Hold on. Take a deep breath. One really important fact to remember is that you are a work in progress. You weren't born knowing absolutely everything. You can't do absolutely everything in the world perfectly and immediately know how to do it. You will grow and change.

Whether you realize it or not, the Lord God began a good work in you. He's not going to let that good work remain unfinished. Instead, He'll keep working on you every day of your life. If you let Him do His good work in you and with you, you'll change and improve more and more until you become just who He wants you to be.

Father, please help me to be more patient with myself and Your process! I don't like my imperfections. I'm really impatient. Please help me learn to wait on You.

NOT ALONE

You are my hiding place; you will protect me from trouble and surround me with songs of deliverance.

Psalm 32:7 NIV

If you're going through a difficult time, it's easy to feel discouraged and down.

Even when you face your darkest days, you're not alone. If you run to God, He can be your hiding place. He'll be your protection. In fact, He's right here, surrounding you.

Knowing you're not alone can be a huge comfort. Your perspective and hope will change once you realize God will protect you and you can hide yourself in Him.

So how can you run to Him when you're in the middle of trouble? Pray to Him! Tell Him everything you're going through and how it makes you feel. Tell Him what you wish would happen. Then ask Him for His help. Ask Him to give you peace and His direction.

Once you've done that, then step out in faith and believe that He'll make a difference. He will!

Father, it feels so good to know I'm never alone. You are my hiding place! Thank You for surrounding me with protection. I want to rely on You.

INCOMPARABLE GIFTS

God raised us up with Christ and seated us with him in the heavenly realms in Christ Jesus, in order that in the coming ages he might show the incomparable riches of his grace, expressed in his kindness to us in Christ Jesus.

EPHESIANS 2:6–7 NIV

Once you belong in Christ by believing in Him, you're promised to be resurrected like Him, from death to life. When you eventually die, you'll be seated with Him in the heavenly realms.

Both of those things sound pretty amazing, and they are! In fact, you'll never be able to compare anything with how priceless these gifts are. They're riches that are given to you by God's grace. Out of His kindness, He gives you an undeserved gift of forever life with Him.

As you live your life right here and now and make the most of today, you can remember that there's so much more waiting for you—so much that simply can't compare to anything here on earth.

Father, thank You for promising me so much through Jesus! Nothing on this earth can compare with the riches You have stored up for me through grace. You are so kind and over-the-top generous. Thank You!

YOU CAN FIND HIM

"From one man he created all the nations throughout the whole earth. He decided beforehand when they should rise and fall, and he determined their boundaries. His purpose was for the nations to seek after God and perhaps feel their way toward him and find him—though he is not far from any one of us."

ACTS 17:26–27 NLT

When you've played hide-and-seek, has there ever been a time when you couldn't find a hider? As much as you tried seeking, did someone stay hidden until you gave up?

While some people like finding a great hiding spot, God is not like that. On the contrary, God gives people the desire to seek Him, and then He makes it clearly obvious where He can be found. It's like He gives all kinds of hints and clues so you can find Him really easily.

God is not far away from you or from anyone else on this earth. He's not trying His hardest to stay hidden. He wants you to find Him. The wonderful thing is, if and when you seek for Him, you *will* find Him.

Father, I'm so glad Your purpose is for people to find You! Please make Yourself absolutely clear to me.

NEVER REJECTED

"Those the Father has given me will come to me, and I will never reject them. For I have come down from heaven to do the will of God who sent me, not to do my own will. And this is the will of God, that I should not lose even one of all those he has given me, but that I should raise them up at the last day."

JOHN 6:37–39 NLT

Most stores have return policies. If you've made a purchase, typically you can return items for your money back or store credit. There are no returns with God. He won't spend the precious blood of Jesus for you and then change His mind. You're not headed back to the return line.

Jesus promised that if you've come to Him in faith, He will never, ever reject you. And God the Father made sure that Jesus wouldn't lose you. In fact, every single person who believes in Christ will be raised up at the last day. That means you'll never be returned. God won't change His mind. He'll never reject you.

Father, thank You for choosing to accept me. Knowing that You won't change Your mind is such an unbelievable comfort.

REAL LOVE

Since God chose you to be the holy people he loves, you must clothe yourselves with tenderhearted mercy, kindness, humility, gentleness, and patience. Make allowance for each other's faults, and forgive anyone who offends you. Remember, the Lord forgave you, so you must forgive others. Above all, clothe yourselves with love, which binds us all together in perfect harmony.

Colossians 3:12–14 NLT

People in this world talk about loving everyone and treating others with kindness. But it's mostly talk and no action. Are their words and actions very loving or kind? Do they forgive when someone says or does something that's offensive?

God calls His followers to live holy lives trademarked by actual, genuine love. Holy living means forgiving other people even when they say or do something truly awful.

As you live in holiness, let your love shine through your kindness. Be patient and gentle with others and yourself. Humbly remember who you are, and then be willing to show mercy and forgiveness to others. When you live like that, you'll show the world what real love and real kindness are all about.

Father, I love You! I want to obey You! Please work through me to show others Your love, kindness, and forgiveness.

PERFECT PEACE

"Peace I leave with you; my peace I give to you. Not as the world gives do I give to you. Let not your hearts be troubled, neither let them be afraid."

JOHN 14:27 ESV

Peace is freedom from disagreements, quarreling, and fighting. It's the absence of hostilities.

Peace sounds wonderful, but it also seems fairly impossible. Are people actually willing to step aside from their own pride and agendas and egos? Can people willingly let disagreements go?

Jesus knew the world promoted a different peace than He offered. He knew that as people dealt with disagreements and faced the consequences of different opinions, worldly peace wasn't possible. But through Him, peace wasn't just possible; it was promised.

Jesus is in the habit of giving peace to those who love Him and rely on Him. He'll flood your heart with peace in a way that nothing else on this earth can. He gives the gift of perfect peace because that perfect peace is part of Him. And He offers it to you.

Lord Jesus, I want Your peace! Thank You for not giving as the world gives. Thank You for Your wonderful gift of peace.

EVERY MOMENT

You made all the delicate, inner parts of my body and knit me together in my mother's womb. Thank you for making me so wonderfully complex! Your workmanship is marvelous—how well I know it. You watched me as I was being formed in utter seclusion, as I was woven together in the dark of the womb. You saw me before I was born. Every day of my life was recorded in your book. Every moment was laid out before a single day had passed.

Psalm 139:13–16 NLT

Just as the Lord made you in an amazing way, He also planned every day of your life. He knows every moment you've had and every moment you ever will have. This truth is something you'll never be able to fully understand, and that's okay.

God created you to be just the way you are. Even though He knows everything about you—the good, the bad, and the ugly—He still chooses to love you. He chose to call you to Himself. He didn't see every day of your life and give up on you. He will always love you and take delight in you.

Father, I don't understand how You know every single part of me and still choose to love me, but I'm so glad You do! Thank You for creating and choosing me.

PRAYING FOR BLESSINGS

We have not stopped praying for you since we first heard about you. We ask God to give you complete knowledge of his will and to give you spiritual wisdom and understanding. Then the way you live will always honor and please the Lord, and your lives will produce every kind of good fruit. All the while, you will grow as you learn to know God better and better.

COLOSSIANS 1:9–10 NLT

Think about someone you care about very much. You want the best for that person, right? You'd be happy to see them receive good things or do good things. It's natural to want to see loved ones succeed. That's exactly what the apostle Paul was talking about when he wrote a letter to his friends in Colossae.

Paul prayed for his friends all the time, especially for the Lord to bless them in big ways. He asked God to give them complete knowledge of His will, along with spiritual wisdom and understanding. Paul realized that if his friends knew God better, their lives would produce all sorts of wonderful outcomes.

Father, would You please give me complete knowledge of Your will? Please give me spiritual wisdom and understanding too so I can know You better and better.

WHERE'S YOUR TRUST?

Some trust in chariots and some in horses, but we trust in the name of the LORD our God. They are brought to their knees and fall, but we rise up and stand firm.

PSALM 20:7–8 NIV

When you think about your everyday life, where do you place your trust? Do you look to the government for help and peace? Do you trust in your own talents and intelligence? Do possessions or money make you feel safe? Do you feel better about yourself if you have a large circle of friends or a boyfriend?

It's easy to look to other people or possessions or positions to feel safe and comfortable. But all of those things—either living or material possessions—aren't worthy of your trust. In fact, all of those things will fail you. It's not a matter of *if* they'll fail you but *when* they will.

But there's one who is always trustworthy and who will never fail: the Lord. You can trust in Him without ever being disappointed.

Father, I praise You for being worthy of my trust. Please forgive me for the times when I look to other things besides You. I want to turn to You alone!

THE GIFT OF GRACE

For it is by grace you have been saved, through faith—and this is not from yourselves, it is the gift of God—not by works, so that no one can boast.

Ephesians 2:8–9 NIV

Grace sounds like a perfect word to use at church: "Amazing grace! How sweet the sound!" But what exactly does *grace* mean? And what does it mean to be saved by it?

Grace, simply put, means unmerited favor. It's an undeserved gift, a special favor of mercy, or an instance and act of kindness.

If and when you choose to align your life with Christ through faith in Him, this grace—God's grace—saves you. There's absolutely nothing in the world you can do to save yourself. There's no amount of talent or good works or money or status that can save you. The only thing that can and does save you is your faith in Jesus Christ. And it's that faith that opens up God's gift of grace to you.

Father, I don't deserve Your grace or Your forgiveness or Your favor. But You've kindly and generously given it to me anyway. Thank You!

ALWAYS AND FOREVER

Lord, you have been our dwelling place throughout all generations. Before the mountains were born or you brought forth the whole world, from everlasting to everlasting you are God.

Psalm 90:1–2 NIV

Forever is such a hard concept to wrap your mind around, yet God has existed as God forever. He always has been God. He is God. And He always will be God. There's never a moment when He's not God.

You can try to figure out the reality of forever until your head hurts. You also can learn to appreciate the fact that you'll never truly understand or comprehend some things in life. Eternity is just one of those things. But you can choose to believe it in faith. And you can choose to worship God for how amazing He is, for He has been God forever and He will be God forever.

Not only does He exist from everlasting to everlasting, but He is also your dwelling place. That means you exist with Him and in Him. He's with you always and forever!

Father, I praise You. You are infinitely more than I can comprehend. You are God!

HIS OWN IMAGE

So God created mankind in his own image, in the image of God he created them; male and female he created them.

GENESIS 1:27 NIV

In the beginning, God created absolutely everything. Once there had been nothing but God, and then He created everything. And it was good. He creatively created every living thing, but when it came to humans, He did something very different. He created men and women in His own image.

Because God created you in His own image, you bear the Lord's image. And no matter what you think about other people, they were made in God's image too. They might not make choices that glorify the Lord, but they're still His image bearer.

Every single person, living and dead, is made in God's image. Every single person matters to God. Not every single person will choose to spend eternity with Him, but He still calls to every single one in His own special way.

Father, I'll never understand why You created humans in Your own image, but I'm honored that You did. I pray that I'd live a life worthy of an image bearer!

SHOW ME THE WAY

Let the morning bring me word of your unfailing love, for I have put my trust in you. Show me the way I should go, for to you I entrust my life.

PSALM 143:8 NIV

Life is confusing. Sometimes it makes sense and you're confident of what you should do. But other times? Totally uncertain.

Instead of feeling lost in confusion, you don't need to try to muddle through life on your own. You can ask the Lord for guidance. Like the psalmist, when you feel uncertain, simply ask God, "Show me the way I should go!"

Like a shepherd, the Lord will faithfully and gently lead you. He has promised never to leave you. And He'll never forsake you. Instead, when you entrust your life to Him and belong to Him, He will guide you by His unfailing, never-ending love.

Father, it's such a relief to know that You love me so much that I can trust You. Please show me the way I should go!

HIS!

To the L*ORD your God belong the heavens, even the highest heavens, the earth and everything in it.*

DEUTERONOMY 10:14 NIV

If you create an art project, it's all yours, right? You've poured your creativity into it; you've spent time forming it and perfecting it. When you've finished with your creation, you're free to do whatever you please with it, whether you display it proudly, set it aside, or give it away as a gift.

Similarly, what God made belongs to Him. The heavens? They belong to Him. The earth and everything in it? They're His too. He can look at everything with ownership and decide what He'd like to do. Since He's God, His ways are higher than your ways and His thoughts are higher than your thoughts. He can and will make the best decisions.

When you realize this truth, it's humbling, for sure. But instead of feeling discouraged because you're powerless, take the time to praise Him. He has created everything! That's amazing! And everything belongs to Him! He's worthy of your praise!

Father, I praise You for Your power and might. I stand in awe of You and Your creative creation.

FROM WEAK TO STRONG

He gives power to the faint, and to him who has no might he increases strength. Even youths shall faint and be weary, and young men shall fall exhausted; but they who wait for the LORD shall renew their strength; they shall mount up with wings like eagles; they shall run and not be weary; they shall walk and not faint.

ISAIAH 40:29–31 ESV

Ever wish you had an extra burst of strength? Maybe you're exhausted after physical activity. Or after a tough exam, your brain seems completely wiped out. Whenever you work really hard, you naturally feel tired and worn out.

If and when you feel completely spent and exhausted, you don't have to give up. When you feel like all your strength and energy are gone, the Lord will give you power. He'll help by actually strengthening you. You'll be able to do with enthusiasm what He's asked you to do.

This extra boost of energy won't just happen automatically. But when you need to feel energized and refreshed, tell the Lord how you're feeling. Ask Him for strength. Wait for Him, step out in faith, and watch what He'll do!

Father, I really need Your strength. I'm so glad I can rely on You!

HELPING OTHERS IN LOVE

"If anyone gives you even a cup of water because you belong to the Messiah, I tell you the truth, that person will surely be rewarded."

MARK 9:41 NLT

Jesus taught that His followers would be known by their love, but sometimes it can seem tricky to figure out how to show love to someone else.

You don't have to go out of your way in an outrageous act of love to show Jesus' love to someone else. It might be as simple as helping out with a task.

Offering a cup of cold water could be a great, practical way to help someone—so would feeding the hungry, visiting the sick, or sharing clothing with people who have nothing. Another way to show Jesus' love is to invite the lonely to be a part of something—maybe you could invite a new girl to sit with you at lunch or get to know your neighbor a little better.

Watch for people who seem to need help, then bravely step up, get to know them, and see if you can help in any way. You might be surprised with the way God will use you!

Father, please help me realize when people need help, and show me ways to help them.

NOW AND LATER

Surely your goodness and love will follow me all the days of my life, and I will dwell in the house of the Lord forever.

Psalm 23:6 NIV

Choosing to trust in and follow the Lord is a win-win situation for you, both now and later. For now, His love and goodness will follow you not just today or tomorrow but all the days of your life. Every one! Even when you face challenges and feel like giving up. His goodness is still there for you, and His love will travel with you.

As if that's not a huge enough blessing, God has also prepared a forever home for you. You'll get to move in and dwell there—not just visit like you've made it to some fantastic vacation destination for a temporary stay. You'll dwell in His house with Him! That means you can move in and settle down and be with Him. If you think you've experienced His goodness and love here on earth, just wait until you're spending eternity with Him in His house!

Father, thank You for loving me and being so good to me now. And thank You for inviting me to stay with You in Your home forever!

PRAY FIRST

If you need wisdom, ask our generous God, and he will give it to you. He will not rebuke you for asking. But when you ask him, be sure that your faith is in God alone. Do not waver, for a person with divided loyalty is as unsettled as a wave of the sea that is blown and tossed by the wind.

JAMES 1:5–6 NLT

Sometimes life seems so confusing. It's hard to know what's right or wrong, especially if other people disagree with you. And when it's time to make a big decision, so many answers seem like they might be good. But is there one right choice? Or are they all right choices?

When you truly don't know what to do, you don't have to feel completely alone in your decision-making. The Lord loves when you seek wisdom. In faith, ask Him for wise decision-making skills, believing He can and will answer you. Trust Him to guide you, and then step out in faith. Sometimes He'll answer you loud and clear, and other times He'll lead you in quiet trust.

Father, no matter how You lead me, I'm thankful You do lead me. Please guide me! I'd love to make a wise choice!

GIVE ME SOME SHELTER

Whoever dwells in the shelter of the Most High will rest in the shadow of the Almighty. I will say of the Lord, "He is my refuge and my fortress, my God, in whom I trust."

Psalm 91:1–2 niv

When you're outside, you're either under shelter or you're not. If a rainstorm suddenly begins, you'll know if you're not under the protection of a shelter because you'll get soaking wet! Shelters do a fantastic job of protecting people from the elements of nature, whether it's the blazing sun, pouring rain, blustery wind, or icy snow.

Just as physical shelter is essential to your long-term safety and short-term comfort, spiritual shelter is essential too. When you trust in the Lord, you decide you'd like for Him to be your safe place. He becomes your fortress in the middle of battles. He becomes your refuge in the storms of life. You can rest in His shadow. You can find protection in His shelter.

Father, in the storms of life, I really need Your shelter. Thank You for protecting me and comforting me. Lord, I trust in You!

HIGHWAY OF HOLINESS

And a great road will go through that once deserted land. It will be named the Highway of Holiness. Evil-minded people will never travel on it. It will be only for those who walk in God's ways; fools will never walk there. Lions will not lurk along its course, nor any other ferocious beasts. There will be no other dangers. Only the redeemed will walk on it.

Isaiah 35:8–9 NLT

When you follow the Lord, you're set apart from people who choose not to follow Him. And as you start to follow Him, it's as if He sets you on the Highway of Holiness. You don't have to worry about facing dangers or fools there—only believers in the Lord will follow the path of holy living.

Holy living means that you're set apart for God. You're His, and not the world's. While others around you focus on the world's values and beliefs and current trends, they're missing out on what's lasting and true. Instead of being pulled off God's highway, keep your eyes fixed on Him and follow after Him!

Father, please help me follow You faithfully! I don't want to be led astray by the cares and desires of this world.

GLORIOUSLY NEW

He will take our weak mortal bodies and change them into glorious bodies like his own, using the same power with which he will bring everything under his control.

Philippians 3:21 NLT

Have you ever wished you could change something about yourself? Maybe you're not completely pleased with the way you look. Or maybe it seems difficult to appreciate your body.

The interesting news is that your body won't stay this same way forever. Sure, you'll grow and change. Your height might stay close to the same, but you'll gain and lose weight. Aside from that normal fluctuation, though, your body will change forever once you die. The Lord will take the body you have now and change it into a glorious body. You won't feel weak anymore. Your body won't be mortal and destined for death. You'll have an immortal body that will last forever.

And how will all of this happen? God will change your body into an everlasting one with His power. You'll get to watch it all happen!

Father, it's a little surprising to think of You transforming my body into something new. However You do it, I know it will be amazing!

SECRETS REVEALED

"The secret things belong to the Lord our God, but the things that are revealed belong to us and to our children forever, that we may do all the words of this law."

Deuteronomy 29:29 ESV

When the Lord set apart the Israelites, He gave His law in the Ten Commandments and the first five books of the Bible, the Pentateuch, to guide them.

The Israelites knew they were supposed to live by the law, obey it, and pass on the truth and instruction to their children. Yet in their human nature, it was easy to slip away from the commandments and disobey.

God knew that as imperfect, sinful people, the Israelites never could keep the law perfectly in their own power. He also knew that His Son, Jesus, could change everything by fulfilling the law. So He sent His Son into the world to be the Savior not just of the Israelites but of all who believe in Him and call on His name. That's the best news ever and should be shared with everyone.

Father, thank You for revealing Your Son to me. I pray that He'll transform my heart.

FILLED WITH JOY

*The Lord has done great things
for us, and we are filled with joy.*
Psalm 126:3 NIV

Take a minute to think of all the great things the Lord has done for you. What special people has He brought into your life? Who do you love? Who loves you? What are some of your favorite things in life—your favorite food? Favorite hobbies? Favorite songs? Favorite ways to spend time with your friends? Favorite animals? Favorite places?

All of those favorite things are really great, and each one is a good gift to you from God. When He brings such good things into your life, whether it's a beautiful sunrise, a hysterically funny conversation with a friend, or a delicious home-cooked meal, enjoy all the joy you feel. As you feel filled with joy, be sure to thank God. He has done great things for you, and He's worthy of your thanks and praise!

Father, thank You so much for all the good things You do for me. You know how happy I am when I experience my favorite people and things. I'm so glad You give preferences so I have my own favorite things!

UNIQUELY YOU

We are God's handiwork, created in Christ Jesus to do good works, which God prepared in advance for us to do.

EPHESIANS 2:10 NIV

When God created you, He formed and fashioned you just the way He wanted you. He gave you a completely unique set of gifts and strengths and talents that no one else in the world has or ever will have. You're uniquely you! He has created you in this most special way for His own special purpose.

He hasn't formed you to keep all your talents hidden away for yourself. He crafted you to be you so you could share your gifts with others. He even created you to do good works—and He has prepared those good works for you already.

Since you have the talents, abilities, and personality, and God has already prepared good works for you to do, now's your chance to go out into the world and use your gifts!

Father, I know You have a plan for me and my life. Thank You! I'm not sure what it is, but please fill me with Your courage to use the gifts You've given me. Please help me do the good things You've already prepared me to do!

RESCUE

The LORD says, "I will rescue those who love me. I will protect those who trust in my name. When they call on me, I will answer; I will be with them in trouble. I will rescue and honor them. I will reward them with a long life and give them my salvation."

PSALM 91:14–16 NLT

Many fairy tales involve a rescue of some kind. Prince Charming rescued Cinderella. Gretel rescued Hansel. Beauty rescued Beast.

A rescue involves some kind of risk; at some point, the hero or heroine puts everything on the line to save the day. This is true in literature, in the plots of many movies, and in real life too.

God promises He will rescue those who love Him. He has done it time and time again, and He will continue to do it.

If you love the Lord, He promises to rescue you. If you trust in His name, He will protect you. When you call on Him, He will answer. When you go through trouble, He will be with you. The Lord will rescue you, honor you, and reward you.

Father, I'm so glad You're my rescuer. I need You!

TRUST FALL

So, my dear brothers and sisters, this is the point: You died to the power of the law when you died with Christ. And now you are united with the one who was raised from the dead. As a result, we can produce a harvest of good deeds for God.

Romans 7:4 NLT

If you've ever done a trust fall, you know how difficult it can be to relax yourself to the point of falling backward, hoping that someone will catch you. Sometimes choosing to follow Jesus can feel like that. Can you trust Him? Will He catch you once you fall?

When you put all your trust in Jesus, He *does* catch you. And He doesn't just catch you, but He unites Himself with you so that you belong to Him. You're His. You don't have to worry about Him judging you according to strict standards. And you won't have to worry about being alone or working so hard in your own strength. Once you trust Him, He'll work in your life in a beautiful way and help you produce an amazing harvest of good deeds.

Lord Jesus, I trust You completely!

THE SWEET PERFUME OF JESUS

But thanks be to God, who in Christ always leads us in triumphal procession, and through us spreads the fragrance of the knowledge of him everywhere. For we are the aroma of Christ to God among those who are being saved and among those who are perishing, to one a fragrance from death to death, to the other a fragrance from life to life.

2 Corinthians 2:14–16 ESV

Scents can be a funny thing. Some of your favorite scents in the whole world can smell less than appealing to someone else. One amazing smell to one person might bring up less than ideal memories for someone else.

Just as many things in life give off scents, your life does too. If you love and follow Christ, your life will smell like His aroma. It's nothing you do on your own; it just happens naturally.

For people who choose not to follow Jesus? His scent is repulsive. But for other believers, your life will smell like the sweet perfume of Jesus. Like a wonderfully fresh scent, you'll smell like life.

Jesus, I praise You! You're living! I want to give off Your fragrance wherever I go.

FOREVER

He will swallow up death forever! The Sovereign Lord will wipe away all tears. He will remove forever all insults and mockery against his land and people. The Lord has spoken!

Isaiah 25:8 NLT

If and when you have a bad day (or a bad week!), it's easy to focus on the negative. Wrongs done to you seem magnified. Little mistakes feel so much bigger. Sometimes all the bad things pile up so that you end up crying over the littlest matter.

These bad days and frustrations won't last forever. In fact, a day is coming when everything awful will be gone. Death will be a thing of the past. Crying will be gone. In fact, the Lord Himself will wipe away every tear. Insults and mockery? All of that will be gone too.

If it sounds too good to be true, just wait for it. It will happen! The Lord has spoken—He will surely do it!

Lord God, it's so wonderful to think that tears and insults and death never were part of Your plan. And it's even better to realize that You'll do away with them all. Thank You for Your comfort and forever peace!

YOUR KEEPER

The LORD watches over you—the LORD is your shade at your right hand; the sun will not harm you by day, nor the moon by night. The LORD will keep you from all harm—he will watch over your life; the LORD will watch over your coming and going both now and forevermore.

PSALM 121:5–8 NIV

Even if you tend to be brave, you'll eventually reach a point where you need to face your fears with courage.

When you do recognize you're afraid, it's okay. Acknowledge your fear instead of trying to stuff it deep inside or shy away. Then remind yourself that the Lord watches over you. He watches over and protects you during the day and all night long. He will guide you and work in you even in the scariest times. You can keep pressing on in faith, knowing that He will keep you from harm. He will watch over you and work in your life.

Father, when I'm afraid and it seems like everything is going wrong, help me to remember Your care and to trust in Your protection. Thank You for watching over me!

GLORY TO GOD

Now all glory to God, who is able, through his mighty power at work within us, to accomplish infinitely more than we might ask or think.

Ephesians 3:20 NLT

Have you ever thought about glorifying God or bringing glory to His name? Have you ever wondered what in the world that even means? *Glorify* means to give honor, high praise, and worship to something, or in the case of God, *someone*! And bringing glory means to bring great honor, praise, renown, or distinction.

God is worthy of being glorified, praised, and worshipped because He's amazing! He can do things no one else could ever do. And He can and will accomplish much more in you and through you than you can even imagine. You wouldn't even be able to think to ask about some of the amazing things He'll do in your life.

Not only is that super exciting, but it also makes Him so very worthy of your praise and worship.

Lord God, I come before You in worship. I praise You! I thank You for doing so much more in my life than I could ever dream.

RADIANCE

Those who look to him are radiant;
their faces are never covered with shame.
PSALM 34:5 NIV

You might have heard that you should never look directly at the sun because its brightness and radiance could harm your eyes. The sun is so brilliant and bright that it naturally makes you squint on a really sunny day.

Just as the sun is radiant, the more time you spend with God, the more radiant you will become. God is infinitely more radiant than our solar system's sun. And His radiance naturally rubs off on you the more you get to know Him.

Take some time today to read your Bible. (Wondering what to read? Try one of the psalms!) Read a few verses and think over what you've observed. Consider how you could apply it to your life. Then pray about what you've read and considered. As you keep doing that day after day, the Lord won't seem so distant. He'll be close to you—and the closer you get, the more radiant you'll be.

Lord, I want to spend more time with You!
I want to look to You for everything!

GONE

Those who belong to Christ Jesus have nailed the passions and desires of their sinful nature to his cross and crucified them there.

GALATIANS 5:24 NLT

The temptation to sin can seem so strong. In fact, sometimes it seems like it's uncontrollable. At times it feels like you're compelled to give in and do what you know is wrong.

If you belong to Christ, you don't have to give in to temptation. In fact, Jesus will give you the strength to stand up against sin. The Bible says that you've nailed your passions and sinful urges to the cross. Those drives and desires are crucified—they're dead. They don't have a hold over you anymore.

Instead of dwelling on the temptations that seem so strong, dwell on the fact that Jesus died so you wouldn't have to be a slave to sin anymore. You're free from the power of sin. Even if and when it seems like it could entice you, remember that it holds no power over you. Your drive to sin? It's gone!

Lord Jesus, thank You for freedom from sin! Thank You for dying so that my sins wouldn't have a hold over me anymore!

KNOWING YOUR HEART

We do not know what we ought to pray for, but the Spirit himself intercedes for us through wordless groans. And he who searches our hearts knows the mind of the Spirit, because the Spirit intercedes for God's people in accordance with the will of God.

Romans 8:26–27 NIV

Have you ever felt so confused that you couldn't even put words to your feelings? Not being able to clarify your thoughts and emotions can be frustrating, but it's a completely normal part of life, no matter your age.

Just as it's not always easy to know what you're thinking or feeling, sometimes you don't know how to pray either. The amazing news is that the Holy Spirit knows you so well that you don't need to tell Him how you're feeling. He knows. He has an amazing way of searching your heart and knowing just what you're experiencing. He knows what grieves you and what brings you joy. Be grateful that He knows just how to step in and plead on your behalf. He knows you well and loves you very much!

Holy Spirit, I don't praise You enough. I'm so glad You know my heart and do what's best for me. I worship You!

ALL THINGS

We know that in all things God works for the good of those who love him, who have been called according to his purpose.

Romans 8:28 NIV

You might have heard the truth of Romans 8:28 before: In all things God works for the good of those who love Him. It can be hard to believe though, especially if you're in the middle of an awful time. When you hear heartbreaking news or you're seriously ill or you're extremely disappointed, it seems like nothing good could come from the situation.

Yet God is working good. Even when it doesn't seem possible, God does work all things together for good for those who love Him. If you've been called by Him, according to His purpose, He is working all situations out for your good.

Rest in that truth, even on your worst days. God is for you!

Father, I'm glad I can trust You even and especially on my worst days. Please give me a glimmer of hope and show me something good in my toughest moments. I trust You!

NEAR TO GOD

For behold, those who are far from you shall perish; you put an end to everyone who is unfaithful to you. But for me it is good to be near God; I have made the Lord God my refuge, that I may tell of all your works.

Psalm 73:27–28 ESV

When you have a really good conversation with a friend, it's natural to get closer together. Deep conversations don't happen when you're farther apart and need to yell to be heard. In fact, you can miss a lot of what someone is saying if you're not close enough.

In the same way, if you're going to have a close, meaningful relationship with God, you need to be near Him. If you're far away, you'll never get a chance to really know Him. And if you stay far away, you make it obvious to Him that you're not trying to get to know Him.

Build your relationship with God by getting close to Him. When you spend time with Him, He'll become your refuge, your safe place, and your closest friend.

Father, I don't want to wait to get close to You—I want to start today.

IN YOUR MIDST

"The Lord your God is in your midst, a mighty one who will save; he will rejoice over you with gladness; he will quiet you by his love; he will exult over you with loud singing."

Zephaniah 3:17 ESV

If something is in your midst, it's right in the middle of everything. Some people like to be in the midst of the action. (And others don't!)

Did you realize that the Lord your God is in your midst? He's in the middle of everything in your life. He's in the middle of all your action. But He's not just a quiet bystander who observes everything. He will save you. He's mighty enough to do that! He will rejoice over you with gladness. He will quiet you by His love. He will rejoice over you with loud singing.

The Lord has promised to shower you with His love, cheer you on, and defend you and your cause. He's your number one fan, and He's always in your midst.

Father, it's amazing that You love me so much and are always cheering me on and wanting what's best for me. Thank You!

ALWAYS LISTENING

I love the Lord, for he heard my voice;
he heard my cry for mercy. Because he turned his ear to me, I will call on him as long as I live.

Psalm 116:1–2 niv

Have you ever tried to get someone else's attention, but they just won't listen to you? Even if they notice that you're talking, they don't fully pay attention. It doesn't matter what you say; they just don't listen.

That kind of refusal to listen never happens with the Lord. He hears your voice. He turns His ear to you. He hears your cries for mercy. When you have something to say, He's listening. He pays attention. He focuses on what you share with Him.

If you know someone cares so deeply for you that He listens to whatever you have to say, no matter when you say it, you should keep talking to Him. Keep sharing what's on your heart and on your mind. He'll listen. And He'll respond out of love.

Lord, it's such a relief to know You listen to me! Thank You for caring so much about me that You pay attention to what I have to say.

LIVE IN HIS REST

Then Jesus said, "Come to me, all of you who are weary and carry heavy burdens, and I will give you rest. Take my yoke upon you. Let me teach you, because I am humble and gentle at heart, and you will find rest for your souls. For my yoke is easy to bear, and the burden I give you is light."

MATTHEW 11:28–30 NLT

Do you ever feel tired of facing troubles and stresses? When you get frustrated and it seems like everything or everyone turns against you, do you start to feel weary? If you think about problems either in your own life or around the world, does it all feel like a heavy burden?

Jesus knew this life would weigh you down. But He came to ease your burden. He came to bring you rest.

In His gentle, humble way, Jesus offers a life that doesn't weigh you down. He offers a freedom you can't find in anything or anyone else. His freedom is light and easy because it brings your soul rest. Through Jesus you can live, thrive, and be refreshed in His rest.

Jesus, thank You for offering me rest. I pray I'll choose to find it in You.

NOT SURPRISING

Dear friends, don't be surprised at the fiery trials you are going through, as if something strange were happening to you. Instead, be very glad—for these trials make you partners with Christ in his suffering, so that you will have the wonderful joy of seeing his glory when it is revealed to all the world.

1 PETER 4:12–13 NLT

Just because someone else opposes your belief doesn't make your belief wrong—it just means you have a difference of opinion.

Not everyone will agree with you when you align yourself with Christ. In fact, facing trials because of His beliefs and teachings shouldn't come as a shock. Of all people, Jesus faced opposition. He knew He was the Son of God, and He wasn't afraid to admit it—even when it cost Him His life. Just as Jesus suffered when He stood up for truth, you can expect to suffer for the sake of truth too. But when you suffer, you can be glad—it means you're like Jesus! You've become His partner in suffering. While that sounds pretty harsh to experience, the amazing news is that all of your suffering will end in joy.

Jesus, I believe in You! I know You're true. Please prepare me to suffer for You and Your truth.

EVERY NEED!

My God will meet all your needs according to the riches of his glory in Christ Jesus.

PHILIPPIANS 4:19 NIV

When you belong to the Lord, you can look forward to the amazing gift of forever life with Him. But while you're here on earth, He doesn't forget about you or leave you on your own. Since you belong to Him—not only here and now but also in the future—He takes care of you in a very generous way.

In God's love and care for you, He supplies every need of yours. You don't need to ask Him ahead of time—He knows what you need even before you ask. And He'll meet every single one of your needs according to His riches in glory. He'll liberally supply them for you so you're filled to overflowing.

If you think about that, it's pretty amazing. There's no way to imagine the riches that are found in Christ's glory, yet God is ready to heap them on and shower you with them. What a generous, caring, giving heavenly Father!

Father, not only do You know my needs, but You also meet them by generously pouring out Your gifts on me. Thank You for sharing Your abundance with me!

PICK A SIDE

The Lord is on my side; I will not fear. What can man do to me? The Lord is on my side as my helper; I shall look in triumph on those who hate me.

Psalm 118:6–7 ESV

Have you ever felt the pressure to pick which side to be on? You can try to stay as impartial to a topic as possible, but at some point you'll be asked to make a decision and pick a side. Once a side is chosen, it automatically eliminates the other side—you align yourself with a belief or a person or a way of life.

When asked about you, the Lord chose you to be on His side. He made His decision. He picked *you*. Now that you're on His side, He's ready and willing to help you. If and when people fight you, know that God is on your side. If your opponents try to say or do hurtful things to you, know that God is with you. You don't have to fear. You don't have to worry and wonder what might happen. Without a doubt, the Lord is your defender.

Lord, thank You for picking me to be on Your side! It's such a comfort and relief to know You're for me!

ARE YOU CONNECTED?

"Remain in me, as I also remain in you. No branch can bear fruit by itself; it must remain in the vine. Neither can you bear fruit unless you remain in me. I am the vine; you are the branches. If you remain in me and I in you, you will bear much fruit; apart from me you can do nothing."

JOHN 15:4–5 NIV

After a windstorm, try picking up fallen branches. Keep the sticks for a while and watch to see if they start sprouting new leaves. You can watch those branches for a long time and nothing will change—well, unless the leaves wither and fall off.

Just like a branch can't grow or thrive or bear fruit if it's not connected to an actual living tree, you can't thrive or bear fruit for the Lord if you're not connected to Him. As much as you hope to be productive in your own strength, it just won't happen. You can't bear fruit unless you remain in Him. Instead of being disappointed that you can't be productive in your own power and strength, be thankful that through Christ He will help you bear much fruit.

Jesus, I want to remain in You! Please help me bear much fruit and do much for You!

LISTEN TO HIS WORDS

"So is my word that goes out from my mouth: It will not return to me empty, but will accomplish what I desire and achieve the purpose for which I sent it."

Isaiah 55:11 NIV

Did you know that God's Word is living and active? According to Hebrews 4:12 it is, and it also judges the thoughts and attitudes of the heart. That can't be said of any other piece of literature!

Just as amazingly, God's Word doesn't return empty. When you hear the Bible, the Lord will use it to achieve a certain purpose. His Word will be used to accomplish what He desires.

The Bible isn't a randomly chosen group of stories. It's truth, and God uses it to teach you, correct you, train you, and equip you for life. The more you listen to it, read it, and obey it, the more deeply it will change you!

Father, thank You so much for Your Word! Please use it in my life to accomplish Your purposes.

PERFECT POWER

He said to me, "My grace is sufficient for you, for my power is made perfect in weakness." Therefore I will boast all the more gladly of my weaknesses, so that the power of Christ may rest upon me.

2 Corinthians 12:9 ESV

Some days you feel like you lack the strength to do what you need to do. When you're asked to do something you're not crazy about doing, it's easy to feel like your energy is depleted. And even if you're really excited about something, you might feel like you're in over your head. You simply have too much to think about or do, or you realize you don't feel talented enough to accomplish what needs to be done.

Whatever the situation, know this: Jesus' power is made perfect in your weakness. When you're weak, He is strong. And when you can't do something on your own and you ask Him for help, He will help—every single time. The power of Christ will rest on you when you're weak. That's way more power than you could ever produce on your own!

Lord Jesus, thank You for giving me strength! Please help me remember that when I am weak, You are strong.

HE KNEW

My frame was not hidden from you, when I was being made in secret, intricately woven in the depths of the earth.

Psalm 139:15 ESV

Long before your mother even knew you existed, God knew. He began making you in secret, intricately weaving your body together. He had a master plan and knew just what you needed to be you. No one else in the world has ever looked or sounded or thought like you, and no one ever will. No one has ever had your unique set of gifts and talents, and no one ever will. You're uniquely you, and God created you to be just the way you are!

Just as the Lord knew His plans for you and the way He wanted to create you even before you were born, He certainly knows you now! Not a moment goes by when He isn't thinking of you. You're never alone, even if you feel like it. From your best days to your worst days, the Lord knows what you're experiencing, and He wants His absolute best for you.

Father, thank You for knowing exactly who I am and choosing to love me anyway.

LIVING IN LIGHT

For once you were full of darkness, but now you have light from the Lord. So live as people of light!

Ephesians 5:8 NLT

Throughout life, certain situations involve absolutes, where you're either one thing or another. You're either awake or asleep. You're either in school or out of school. You either have a job or don't have a job. You either know Jesus or don't know Jesus. You're either in darkness or in light.

When it comes to knowing Jesus, there's no way to walk or live in Him unless He's in you. No Jesus? No life and no light from the Lord. But if you do know Jesus, you do have life and light in Him.

If Jesus really is in you, it's time to start walking in His ways. That includes obedience to what He asks. You'll obey and serve Him out of love. You'll choose to do what He has asked you to do, even when it makes you feel uncomfortable or even when you need to put your own will aside. If Jesus really is in you, it's time to let His light shine in your life!

Lord Jesus, I love You and want to live in Your light!

MINDFULNESS

When I consider your heavens, the work of your fingers, the moon and the stars, which you have set in place, what is mankind that you are mindful of them, human beings that you care for them?

Psalm 8:3–4 NIV

Have you taken time to look up at the night sky? Have you stopped to consider the moon and the stars? Look at them. Those tiny stars are trillions of miles away, yet you can see them sparkle brightly from where they are set in just the place the Lord designed.

Creation holds so many secrets we'll never discover, yet God knows exactly how He created everything. He also knows why He created everything in particular ways.

When you consider how vast creation is yet how intricately detailed things are, from the microscopic cells in your body to the beautiful petals of a flower, it's astounding to know God cares so much for mankind. Out of all of His creation, He created humans in His image. And He sent His only Son to this world as a human on a rescue mission. That's a mindful, compassionate God who loves you completely!

Father, thank You for caring for me! Your creation is beautiful. Thank You for choosing to love human beings the way You do!

TRANSFORMER

Whenever anyone turns to the Lord, the veil is taken away. Now the Lord is the Spirit, and where the Spirit of the Lord is, there is freedom. And we all, who with unveiled faces contemplate the Lord's glory, are being transformed into his image with ever-increasing glory, which comes from the Lord, who is the Spirit.

2 Corinthians 3:16–18 niv

If you've ever watched makeover shows, you know that whether it's a home or someone's style that's getting updated, the big reveal is usually pretty drastic! It's fun to see proof of before and after a transformation.

When you ask Jesus to become Lord of your life, you experience your own makeover. Your life is one way before you come to know Jesus. But once you commit your life to Him, you experience freedom. Suddenly you're able to reflect His glory. That makeover process transforms your heart and soul. It also can change your appearance, as you experience His joy and peace in a brand-new way. Even if you can't see it with your own eyes, you'll feel and look a lot different during your own big reveal!

Father, being transformed by You is such a gift. Thank You for making me over through faith in Jesus!

MORE THAN WORKS

When the goodness and loving kindness of God our Savior appeared, he saved us, not because of works done by us in righteousness, but according to his own mercy, by the washing of regeneration and renewal of the Holy Spirit, whom he poured out on us richly through Jesus Christ our Savior.

Titus 3:4–6 ESV

It can be easy to think you deserve something. When you treat people with kindness, you think you deserve kindness in return. If you study hard for a test, you think you deserve a good grade. When you do good things, you think you deserve favor.

But that's not the way God looks at things. Even if you try hard to please Him through doing good things, you won't earn favor with the Lord.

Instead of checking on how much good you've done, the Lord looks at your heart and what you believe. Do you believe in His Son? Through Jesus' goodness and love, He saves you then regenerates and renews you through His Holy Spirit. You simply can't do those things on your own. But He can.

Lord, thank You for Your goodness and love! Thank You for saving me according to Your own mercy!

SUCH A TIME AS THIS

"If you keep silent at this time, relief and deliverance will rise for the Jews from another place, but you and your father's house will perish. And who knows whether you have not come to the kingdom for such a time as this?"

ESTHER 4:14 ESV

Regardless of whether you appreciate living at this moment in history, one thing is certain: God planned for you to live right here and right now. He planned for you to live and think and speak in this current world. He knew that out of all moments throughout time, this would be your moment to shine.

Today's world needs to hear your voice. People around you need to know your opinion. And as you share it with the love of Christ, you can start making a difference in the people around you. Just as Queen Esther was encouraged by her cousin Mordecai, his wise words apply to you too: "Who knows whether you have not come. . .for such a time as this?"

Father, thank You for putting me right here right now. Please help me bravely stand up for Your truth today.

ALL YOU NEED

God will generously provide all you need. Then you will always have everything you need and plenty left over to share with others. As the Scriptures say, "They share freely and give generously to the poor. Their good deeds will be remembered forever."

2 Corinthians 9:8–9 NLT

Have you stopped to think about the way God gives you so much? He's actually the one who gives you absolutely everything you need. Everything you think you might deserve or receive as a gift from someone else is provided by your heavenly Father. He uses different ways to provide, but He still makes sure you're taken care of very well.

After you thank Him for providing everything for you, share your wealth! Use what you need, but when you have extra—whether it's food or clothing or other possessions—copy the Lord's generosity and share your good gifts with someone else. As you share freely and give generously, your life and giving will look more and more like the Lord's.

Father, thank You for generously providing all I need! It's such a relief to know You'll always give me everything I need so that I even have plenty left over to share with others.

READY TO START?

Therefore, since we have been made right in God's sight by faith, we have peace with God because of what Jesus Christ our Lord has done for us. Because of our faith, Christ has brought us into this place of undeserved privilege where we now stand, and we confidently and joyfully look forward to sharing God's glory.

Romans 5:1–2 NLT

When you used to play board games like Candy Land, each game began with the first space. Once you were ready to play and your piece was placed on the space marked "Start," you could proceed by drawing cards.

In much the same way, belief in Christ is the start of your Christian life. Faith is the starting space you need before you can continue. Once you believe through faith, you're ready to start the rest of your journey of a life lived in peace with God. Your new life includes privilege with God that you don't deserve. And you can joyfully and confidently wait for the big finish: living in the presence of the living God in all His glory.

Father, I want to start my life with You, and through Jesus I want to be at peace with You. I trust in Him!

SHEEPISH

Come, let us bow down in worship,
let us kneel before the Lord our Maker;
for he is our God and we are the people
of his pasture, the flock under his care.

Psalm 95:6–7 NIV

Sheep follow their shepherds anywhere and everywhere. They trust their shepherd to feed them and lead them. In fact, they respond only to their shepherd's call.

Just as sheep know and listen to their shepherd, you can choose to know and obey the Lord. His followers are like His sheep. Jesus is the good shepherd—so good that He laid down His life for His sheep. As a leader and shepherd that loving and sacrificial, He is worthy of all your praise. You can bow down to Him in worship. You can kneel before Him knowing that He is your Lord. He is your Maker. He is your God. He is your shepherd.

Lord Jesus, I worship You! Thank You for leading me so well. And thank You for giving Your life so I might live forever. Please help me stick near You like a sheep since You are the good shepherd.

WALK WORTHY

Walk in a manner worthy of the calling to which you have been called, with all humility and gentleness, with patience, bearing with one another in love, eager to maintain the unity of the Spirit in the bond of peace.

EPHESIANS 4:1–3 ESV

God called you and chose you to belong to Him. Not everyone gets that favor! Because He chose you, it's only appropriate that you live in a way to reflect that gift.

If you're wondering what kind of a life shows that you recognize and value your calling, the Bible details it in Ephesians 4: Set aside your pride and live a humble life. Be gentle and persevere instead of being harsh or impatient. Out of love and for the sake of peace, tolerate and accept others as an attempt to stay unified.

Walking worthy of your calling in Christ definitely is different than the way most people live. Out of your thankfulness and love for Him, choose to live the way He asks!

Lord Jesus, it's not always easy to live the way You'd like me to live. But I want to live full of Your love, patience, and kindness. Please help me reflect Your humility and gentleness to everyone around me!

LOVED AND FORGIVEN

For as high as the heavens are above the earth,
so great is his love for those who fear him;
as far as the east is from the west, so far has
he removed our transgressions from us.

PSALM 103:11–12 NIV

When you belong to Christ, God looks at you differently. Not only does He love you and shower you with His favor, but He also pours out His forgiveness on you.

In fact, He loves you so much that the Bible describes the greatness as being as high as the heavens are above the earth. And His forgiveness? Through Jesus He has removed your sins as far as the east is from the west. Just take one step outside and look to the east. Then turn around and look to the west. Both directions seem to run in separate directions forever, right? That's the magnitude of your forgiveness.

Lord, I can't fully comprehend the scope of Your love or Your forgiveness. But I'm so grateful for both of them! Thank You so much for loving me infinitely more than I can imagine and for forgiving me infinitely more than I deserve.

HIS MISSION

"For God did not send his Son into the world to condemn the world, but in order that the world might be saved through him. Whoever believes in him is not condemned, but whoever does not believe is condemned already, because he has not believed in the name of the only Son of God."

JOHN 3:17–18 ESV

Have you ever thought about why God the Father would send His only Son into the world? Jesus could have stayed in heaven forever to experience the honor, praise, and worship He rightfully deserves. But He humbled Himself, came to this earth as a baby, and lived a life of humility instead of riches or royalty.

Jesus was sent on this mission for one reason: to save those who would trust in Him. He wasn't sent to condemn the world. In fact, the world already was condemned, thanks to the fall of man back in Genesis.

Jesus was sent on a rescue mission. And once you believe in the name of the only Son of God, you'll be rescued from condemnation. You'll be saved and set free through your trust in Him.

Jesus, thank You for being so willing to come and rescue those who believe in You!

SPECIAL TREATMENT

The Lord is close to all who call on him, yes, to all who call on him in truth. He grants the desires of those who fear him; he hears their cries for help and rescues them. The Lord protects all those who love him, but he destroys the wicked.

Psalm 145:18–20 NLT

When you belong to the Lord, you get special treatment. (Who doesn't like that!?) When you belong to Him, naturally you call on Him, fear Him out of great respect, and love Him with all your heart.

Because of this, the Lord is close to you. He'll hear your cries for help and rescue you. He'll grant your desires. And He'll protect you.

People who don't love or honor or acknowledge Jesus? They don't get His special treatment. People who are wicked? Eventually they'll face destruction.

Just as you're more willing to listen and respond to someone you know and love very well, the Lord does the same with you. He responds to you with much love and concern because you're His.

Lord, I do love You! And I come to You today with reverent fear. Thank You for taking such special care of me.

FREE TO SERVE

Live as people who are free, not using your freedom as a cover-up for evil, but living as servants of God.

1 Peter 2:16 ESV

Through Jesus you experience immense freedom. Since you're not a slave to sin anymore, you don't have to feel compelled to do what's wrong. You can choose to do what's right!

Out of your freedom, don't keep sinning to take advantage of God's grace. Instead, use your time and choices to serve the Lord. This service will spill out of your love for Him. Are you truly grateful for all He has done for you? Show it by the way you serve Him!

Love looks like joyfully serving those you love. You may not always enjoy doing certain things, but you can do those undesirable tasks in love. For example, your parents probably didn't always love changing your dirty diapers when you were a baby, but they did it out of their intense love for you. Similarly, you can choose to serve God out of love, no matter what the task might be.

Father, I love You! I'm thankful You saved me from the slavery of sin. I want to serve You out of my love for and devotion to You!

GO RIGHT IN

Dear brothers and sisters, we can boldly enter heaven's Most Holy Place because of the blood of Jesus. By his death, Jesus opened a new and life-giving way through the curtain into the Most Holy Place. And since we have a great High Priest who rules over God's house, let us go right into the presence of God with sincere hearts fully trusting him. For our guilty consciences have been sprinkled with Christ's blood to make us clean, and our bodies have been washed with pure water.

Hebrews 10:19–22 NLT

In the Old Testament, going from the temple's holy place to the most holy place to make a blood sacrifice was an Israelite high priest's sacred duty just once a year.

But matters changed with Jesus. At His crucifixion, the curtain between the holy place and most holy place was torn in two. He was the blood sacrifice that would cleanse us from our sins and allow us to enter into the holy God's presence.

Jesus now sits as the great High Priest who rules over God's house and is the one who steps in on your behalf. Today, because of Him, you can go right into God's presence.

Jesus, it's amazing that You are the great High Priest. Thank You for saving me and interceding for me!

LIVING IN HIS LIGHT

But let us who live in the light be clearheaded, protected by the armor of faith and love, and wearing as our helmet the confidence of our salvation.

1 Thessalonians 5:8 NLT

When you think about day and night, you notice an obvious difference between the two: light. During the day, things are light because of the sun. But once the sun sets, everything is dark.

Just like the difference between day and night, there's a noticeable contrast between those who believe in Christ and those who don't. Believers live in light because the Light of the World is a part of them. He clearly lights the way. But those who don't believe live in darkness. They stumble around, like being stuck outside in the middle of the night without a flashlight.

If you have the light of Christ, it's important to live like it. Christ protects you in many ways so you're free to live out your faith in a right, pure way without any fear or confusion. He illuminates your life's path with His light. You don't have to fear the darkness!

Jesus, thank You for shining Your light into my heart. I want to trust You completely and show the world I'm living in Your light.

TOGETHER!

How good and pleasant it is when God's people live together in unity!

PSALM 133:1 NIV

If you belong to Christ, it's important to remember that you're not the only one who does. In fact, you're just one member of God's huge family. You have countless sisters and brothers in Christ! Believers from all around the world share a common belief with you: Jesus is alive, and He is Lord of all.

Just as families are stronger when they're united in love, stay united with other believers. As much as it's possible, don't get hung up on your differences. Instead, remember what unifies you: Christ! And try to encourage and support each other because of that unity.

Because you'll get to spend eternity together, now's a perfect time to practice some family unity!

Father God, it's exciting to think that I'm part of Your family along with people from every nationality and culture. Please help me to be a good sister in Christ by seeking ways to be united with other believers.

MEASURING UP

Now these are the gifts Christ gave to the church: the apostles, the prophets, the evangelists, and the pastors and teachers. Their responsibility is to equip God's people to do his work and build up the church, the body of Christ. This will continue until we all come to such unity in our faith and knowledge of God's Son that we will be mature in the Lord, measuring up to the full and complete standard of Christ.

Ephesians 4:11–13 NLT

Have you ever been compared to someone else? Usually it doesn't feel so great to try to measure up to someone else. In fact, comparison can make you feel insecure or uncertain.

Christ has set a standard. (Spoiler alert: It's impossible to meet His standard on your own!) Anyone who believes in Christ is on a lifelong adventure of measuring up to His standard through the power of the Holy Spirit within.

As you mature, God will use other believers in your life to build you up. Welcome that process as you grow in your faith and your knowledge of God, because it will help you measure up to Christ's standard!

Lord, thank You for sending other believers into my life to help me learn and grow!

KINDNESS IS COOL

"Love your enemies! Do good to them. Lend to them without expecting to be repaid. Then your reward from heaven will be very great, and you will truly be acting as children of the Most High, for he is kind to those who are unthankful and wicked. You must be compassionate, just as your Father is compassionate."

Luke 6:35–36 NLT

If someone is mean to you, a natural response is to repay that cruelty. But instead of looking for ways to get a payback, do what God asks you to do, which is something completely different: Love instead of hate. Be kind instead of cruel. Do good instead of evil. Be compassionate instead of nasty.

Loving your enemies is hard. It seems to go against everything that feels natural. But you're not asked to do what's natural. In fact, the Lord will give you power and strength to do what's supernatural. When it feels like kindness is the last thing you want to give, pray for the Lord to help you. Ask to be filled with His compassion and love. Then do good, even to your enemies.

Father, Your ability to love and be kind and compassionate is absolutely amazing. I want to learn from You! Please help me!

A GENEROUS GIVER

From his abundance we have all received one gracious blessing after another.

John 1:16 NLT

Who is the most generous person you know? What makes them particularly generous? How much and how often do they give to others? How does their generosity make you feel—especially if you're on the receiving end?

Take that most generous person and multiply their generosity by about a billion. Even then you won't come close to getting a good picture of the Lord's abundance and generosity.

God gives and gives and gives. It's His character to pour out His blessings on everyone—especially those who belong to Him. A loving earthly father typically gives his child good gifts, but God does even more. And He doesn't just wait until your birthday or holidays to give you something—He gives and gives every day.

When you experience the Lord's generous gifts and blessings, thank Him! Be grateful for the gifts you recognize right away and thank Him when you realize what good gifts His unexpected and unlikely blessings are.

Thank You, Father! You've filled my life with such good gifts.

FORGIVENESS

O Lord, you are so good, so ready to forgive,
so full of unfailing love for all who ask for your help.
Listen closely to my prayer, O Lord; hear my urgent cry.

Psalm 86:5-6 NLT

When you've wronged someone, it's easy to feel embarrassed and ashamed. You feel guilty because you're at fault. You wish you could go back and make things happen differently. Sometimes, in the middle of all your awkwardness, the person you've wronged offers forgiveness. They don't hold a grudge against you, and it's as if nothing ever happened.

Whether you intentionally try or not, you end up wronging God every day. Sinning against God is a daily occurrence. But when you confess your sins and ask God for forgiveness, He willingly forgives. He's good. His love for you never fails. And once He forgives you, He won't hold a grudge.

When you live in God's love and forgiveness, He listens closely to your prayers. He hears your urgent cries. And He responds to you in His great, unfailing love. As awkward as it might feel, come to God and admit your sins. Ask for His forgiveness. Then soak in His great love.

Lord, I confess that I've sinned against You!
Please forgive me and help me become more like You.

A DIFFERENT KIND OF LIFE

Finally, all of you, be like-minded, be sympathetic, love one another, be compassionate and humble.

1 Peter 3:8 NIV

When you choose to follow God, you choose to live differently than those around you. Through His strength, you'll set aside natural tendencies and reactions that come from pride. You'll stop focusing on your own comfort and interests. Instead, when you realize and embrace the fact that God is God and you're not, your pride will start to vanish and you'll see yourself humbly and accurately.

You'll start to look at other people differently too. Instead of judging them, you'll try to understand what they're facing and be more sympathetic and compassionate. Through the Holy Spirit's power, you'll try to see things from other people's perspectives. And you'll be able to love people really well. You won't just say that you're a loving person—you'll actually love in a way that comes only from God.

Father God, I want to live differently than so many people in this world who say one thing and do another thing. I want to authentically love well, just like You do. Through Your Holy Spirit, please help me to be more like You!

IN TIMES OF TROUBLE

God is our refuge and strength,
always ready to help in times of trouble.
Psalm 46:1 NLT

It's easy to stress out when you feel bullied or trapped, either by unfair situations or people with cruel intentions. When you know you're up against opposition and don't know what to do, it's a perfect time to tell everything to the Lord. Tell Him your cares. Tell Him your worries. Talk to Him about your fears and concerns and doubts. Go ahead and tell Him all that you're thinking, including all the what-ifs that keep you up at night.

As you tell God everything, ask for His help. Since He's Lord of all creation, He has so much more power than you can begin to comprehend. He's able and willing to protect you from danger and hardship. If you run to Him, He'll be your shelter in the storms of life. He's always ready to help you in times of trouble. And He's always ready to be your strength, even when it feels like you don't have any.

Father God, I run to You! I need Your help. And I need Your strength and protection to make it through my troubles today.

REGARDLESS

"We believe that we are all saved the same way, by the undeserved grace of the Lord Jesus."

Acts 15:11 NLT

This world is filled with all kinds of people who believe all kinds of things. Each person is unique. All of our differences can be celebrated. Yet regardless of who a person is or where each person comes from, there's only one way to be saved: by the grace of Jesus. Regardless of what a person does—whether they focus on doing good or focus on pleasing themselves—not a single person deserves Jesus' grace.

This means the playing field is leveled. You don't have an advantage over anyone else. Yet no matter where you come from, who you're related to, or how you've been raised, you have just as much need for Jesus and His saving power as anyone else you see. Through faith, it's Jesus' grace that saves you. Regardless of who you are, you need Jesus.

Lord Jesus, I need You! I know I don't deserve Your grace, but I'm so thankful for it. I trust You and believe You alone can save me!

THE PERFECT PERSON FOR YOU

Your eyes saw my unformed body; all the days ordained for me were written in your book before one of them came to be.

PSALM 139:16 NIV

Have you ever wished someone would know all of you, from your strengths to your flaws, and still accept you completely? Maybe you wish you had a best friend you could trust with all of your hopes and dreams. Or maybe you wish for a romantic relationship and hope that someday you'll find a soul mate.

Living, breathing, actual people can't meet all of your needs. As much as you hope for a soul mate, no one person will ever fulfill you. The more people you get to know, the more you'll realize this.

Instead of being disappointed with people's limitations time and time again, turn to the Limitless One. He created you. He has planned all the days of your life. He knows and loves you completely.

My Lord and my God, I praise You! It's amazing that You know me completely and absolutely love me. I am humbled by Your goodness and faithfulness.

NO PENALTY

Yet God, in his grace, freely makes us right in his sight. He did this through Christ Jesus when he freed us from the penalty for our sins.

ROMANS 3:24 NLT

Whether you're playing sports or concentrating on school rules or obeying the law, you don't want to get a penalty. Getting punished or facing consequences for breaking a law or rule is never enjoyable.

Disobedience always results in consequences, no matter the situation. When you sin, you deserve a penalty.

The wild thing, though, is this: God knows that the penalty for sinning is harsh. In fact, the penalty is forever separation from Him. Since He created you and loves you, He offers you a way out of the punishment and penalty. When you believe in Jesus, God makes you right in His sight. Jesus took care of your penalty. Your punishment is paid for—you don't have to worry about anything.

God has given you this huge, undeserved gift. But like any gift, it's not yours until you receive it and open it up. What are you waiting for?

Father, thank You for making me right in Your sight through Jesus! I'm relieved I don't have to worry about the penalty for my sins.

FEAR FACTOR

How great is the goodness you have stored up for those who fear you. You lavish it on those who come to you for protection, blessing them before the watching world.

PSALM 31:19 NLT

We live in a world where we're conditioned to think of fear as something to avoid. So what does the Bible mean when it says to fear the Lord?

Fearing the Lord doesn't involve danger. Rather, it means that you respect the Lord with awe and reverence. As you recognize that He's the God of the universe, fearing the Lord simply means you honor and respect Him for who He is.

When you do fear Him, you get plenty of benefits: God stores up goodness for those who fear Him and then lavishes His goodness on them. Plus, according to Proverbs, the fear of the Lord is a fountain of life that leads to rest and satisfaction. It's also the beginning of wisdom.

When you honor and respect God for who He is, He really will bless you before the watching world!

Father, I worship You! You are truly great. I'm in awe that You're Lord of all and still regard me.

WHAT'S AMAZING ABOUT GRACE?

I give thanks to my God always for you because of the grace of God that was given you in Christ Jesus.

1 Corinthians 1:4 ESV

Grace can be defined as unmerited favor—that means it's favor you don't work to earn. God, being the giver of all good gifts, decided to go all out and surprise you with an amazing, undeserved gift: He blesses you instead of cursing you.

You're undeserving of His blessing—everyone is!—yet the Lord chose to give it to you anyway because He's full of love and kindness. The miracle of grace is that God chose to make a way for you to enter a relationship with Him, and that way is through Christ Jesus. When you say yes to Christ, you say yes to accepting God's good gift of grace. You choose to unwrap that gift and make it your own. Once you realize what a priceless gift you now possess, your heart can be filled with thankfulness to your heavenly Father!

My Lord and my God, thank You!
Thank You for Your amazing gift of grace.
Thank You for offering it to me through Jesus.

GET YOUR HEAD IN THE GAME

With minds that are alert and fully sober,
set your hope on the grace to be brought to you
when Jesus Christ is revealed at his coming.

1 Peter 1:13 NIV

While you can experience parts of God's gift of grace right now, you won't get to fully comprehend it until Jesus returns. In the meantime, you have a life to live. And your life will include plenty of choices and daily decisions. How can you live while you're in the middle of waiting?

Peter, one of Jesus' closest friends and followers, shared a practical way to wait: Prepare your mind for action! Stay alert! Mentally get yourself ready.

As you face both big and small challenges every day, how should you respond? How can you demonstrate your love and devotion to Christ in what you say and do?

A lot of your responses call for self-control—a choice not to do or say what you really feel. As you wait for Christ, remember that you're His messenger in this world. Act like one while you wait for Him!

Lord Jesus, it's hard to wait for You! I pray I'll get my head in the game and control myself as I try to be Your example in this world.

LIGHT IN DARKNESS

"I have come into the world as a light, so that no one who believes in me should stay in darkness."

JOHN 12:46 NIV

Think about a time when you've been in total darkness. It's easy to fumble and stumble around when you can't see your surroundings.

Now think about what your dark experience would have been like if you had a flashlight. Totally different, right? You wouldn't have to worry about what might be around you. You'd know how to safely make your way to your destination. You wouldn't fear unknowns that might lurk in the dark.

Without Jesus, this world is a dark, dark place. Everything seems confusing, and nothing seems to make sense without Him. But if you embrace the light of Jesus, you don't have to stay in the darkness anymore! You can know the right way to go. You don't have to worry about stubbing your toe or falling into a dangerous trap. Keep your eyes focused on His light. Instead of wandering back into the darkness, stay close to Him, and He'll safely guide you through this life!

Lord Jesus, I'm so thankful for Your light! You make my life so much better and brighter.

ROOTED IN LOVE

That you, being rooted and grounded in love, may have strength to comprehend with all the saints what is the breadth and length and height and depth, and to know the love of Christ that surpasses knowledge, that you may be filled with all the fullness of God.

EPHESIANS 3:17–19 ESV

If you examine a big tree, you might notice leaves and branches right away. But keep looking, and it's impossible to miss the incredible root system. Roots keep a tree well grounded even when fierce wind gusts and devastating storms pass. They also keep trees watered and nourished.

Just like a tree, you need good roots too, or the storms of life will topple you. But what kind of roots will both sustain you with nourishment and keep you well grounded?

The love of Christ roots and grounds you in an amazing way. It fills you with all the fullness of God so you get an accurate picture of how high and wide and long and deep His love really is. Much like the way you'll never really know how big a tree is unless you're standing right beside it, you won't know the reality of Christ's love until you fully experience it.

Jesus, Your love is amazing. It's wonderful to be loved by You!

PLAYING FAVORITES

If God is for us, who can ever be against us? Since he did not spare even his own Son but gave him up for us all, won't he also give us everything else? Who dares accuse us whom God has chosen for his own? No one—for God himself has given us right standing with himself. Who then will condemn us? No one—for Christ Jesus died for us and was raised to life for us, and he is sitting in the place of honor at God's right hand, pleading for us.

Romans 8:31–34 NLT

What's one of your absolute favorite things? In your eyes, you can't find many (if any) faults in it. Did you know that God has His own list of favorites too? And did you know you're on that list?

Just like you're for your favorite things, God is for you. He has chosen you. No one and nothing can condemn you. He gave the very best He had—His one and only Son!—just for you. He loves you that much.

If the God of the universe is for you (and He is!), absolutely nothing will ever stand in the way of God's never-ending love.

Father God, I'm not sure why You chose me to be one of Your favorites, but I'm so glad You did!

COMMITTED AND STRENGTHENED

"For the eyes of the Lord range throughout the earth to strengthen those whose hearts are fully committed to him."

2 Chronicles 16:9 NIV

From the very beginning of the Bible, it's obvious that God created the world and all that is in it. He created humans, and all throughout His Word, you're reminded of how God sees you and knows you. He knows your heart and He knows your mind. Your thoughts and intentions aren't hidden from Him.

Because God knows all people, He knows exactly who loves Him. And He knows exactly who is committed to Him. He knows when someone only says that they love or believe Him, and He knows when people actually do love Him or believe Him.

If and when God knows your heart is fully committed to Him, He will help you. He'll support you. He'll strengthen you.

O Lord, You know all. You see my heart and You know every detail about me. I pray You'll find me fully committed to You!

CHOSEN AND CALLED

Even before I was born, God chose me and called me by his marvelous grace.

GALATIANS 1:15 NLT

In this world, we are so conditioned to believe we need to earn favor. If we could just work hard enough or know the "right" people or do the right thing, we could get what we want. We might even be worth more in someone else's eyes.

God doesn't think or act or respond to that line of thinking. It doesn't matter how hard you work. You don't have to know the "right" people, and you don't have to do the right thing. Before you were born, God chose you. He chose you when you had absolutely nothing to offer. He chose you long before you could choose Him. He chose you and He called you to be His.

Out of His amazing grace—that precious gift you can't earn and would never deserve—He called you to be His. What you can choose to do is thank and praise Him for His immense favor!

Father! It's amazing to know You chose and called me to be Yours even before I was born. I am humbled by and thankful for Your decision and Your grace.

MORE OF HIM

Don't copy the behavior and customs of this world, but let God transform you into a new person by changing the way you think. Then you will learn to know God's will for you, which is good and pleasing and perfect.

Romans 12:2 NLT

After Adam and Eve gave in to temptation in the garden of Eden and sin entered the world, God's creation quickly fell away from Him.

Because of this, it shouldn't surprise you that the behaviors and customs of most people are centered on themselves instead of the Lord. But when you decide to follow after the Lord, you want to become more like Him and less like the world.

As you seek a life that honors the Lord who created, chose, and saved you, be open to the way He'll change your heart and your mind. Learn from Him, both in prayer and by reading the Bible. As you do, you'll find yourself becoming less and less like the world and more and more like the Lord.

Lord, please give me a new mind and change the way I think so that I'm not copying what the world says or does.

A HELPER

"The Helper, the Holy Spirit, whom the Father will send in my name, he will teach you all things and bring to your remembrance all that I have said to you."

John 14:26 ESV

Trying to figure out how to live like God's daughter can feel confusing and overwhelming. The world screams messages at you to influence your thoughts and decisions. But God's way is so very different from the world's. And sometimes His direction seems more like a quiet whisper you have to strain to hear.

Fortunately, God doesn't make you try to figure out His way on your own. He has given you the Bible for you to read, study, and understand. And He has given you an amazing gift: the Holy Spirit. Once you ask Jesus to be Lord of your life, the Holy Spirit comes to live with you as your Helper. He teaches you the truth. He guides you in the way you should go. He pricks your conscience when you sin. He is God living in you.

Lord, I don't understand how the Holy Spirit can live in me, but I'm grateful You've sent Him to help me! Please help me fully appreciate what a good gift He is.

YOUR INSTRUCTION MANUAL

All Scripture is breathed out by God and profitable for teaching, for reproof, for correction, and for training in righteousness, that the man of God may be complete, equipped for every good work.

2 Timothy 3:16–17 ESV

Have you ever started a big project without any instructions? Unless you were expecting a completely creative result, how did your project turn out?

Most of the time, instruction manuals are really helpful in telling the right way to proceed. Not only do you save time by following instructions, but when you don't have to guess at what to do, you also have a lot less frustration.

Just as directions make tasks easier, the Bible is a fantastic instruction manual. God knew you'd need some help, and His Word is absolutely helpful for all sorts of things. It helps train you in right living so you can be ready and able to do the good works God has prepared for you to do. All you need to do is read it—and follow the instructions!

Father, thank You for Your Word! It's reassuring to know that I don't have to stumble through life on my own. I want to follow Your directions!

SAVE ME!

If you confess with your mouth that Jesus is Lord and believe in your heart that God raised him from the dead, you will be saved. For with the heart one believes and is justified, and with the mouth one confesses and is saved.

ROMANS 10:9–10 ESV

You might have heard that "Jesus saves." But from what does He save you? And how does He save you?

Everyone sins. Sins keep you from a relationship with God; because of them you deserve punishment. But out of His great mercy, God sent Jesus to save you from your own punishment.

The thing is, you have to know that Jesus took your punishment and choose to trust in it. When you do that, you can accept the gift—the fact that He traded His life for yours. You can ask Him to save you and become Lord of your life. You can believe in your heart that He really, truly is Lord. When you do believe in your heart that after Jesus died for you He rose from the dead and is living today, you'll be saved and made right with God. What will you choose?

Jesus, I believe You are my Lord! And I believe that God raised You from the dead and You are alive today. Please save me!

CAN YOU TASTE IT?

Taste and see that the Lord is good.
Oh, the joys of those who take refuge in him!
Psalm 34:8 NLT

What's your favorite flavor? Some people prefer salty foods; others prefer sweet. You might be partial to something sour, or bitter foods might even tempt your taste buds.

Whatever flavor you like to savor, the Lord created them all—and He created an enormous variety of foods for you to enjoy. The next time you eat, slow down and notice the flavors in each bite. What does everything taste like? What tastes really good to you?

As you enjoy each flavorful bite, praise your heavenly Father for giving you vivid senses like taste. Then thank Him for filling your days with foods that taste so unique. He has given a huge variety of flavors, and He has given you a tongue to taste them all. Thank Him and praise Him for those good gifts!

Father God, thank You for food! It's a good gift! When I taste it and like the flavors, I know that You are a good, good God.

IT'S YOUR CHOICE!

"Those who accept my commandments and obey them are the ones who love me. And because they love me, my Father will love them. And I will love them and reveal myself to each of them."

JOHN 14:21 NLT

At times obedience can seem like a painful request. If you want freedom, obeying someone else can feel stifling. But if the person you're obeying is trustworthy, loves you, and ultimately has your best interests in mind, their commands are worth obeying.

While He lived on earth, Jesus talked about the option of obeying His commands. You don't have to obey them, but that decision holds consequences. If you do choose to accept and obey His commands, you're showing Jesus that you love Him. You are showing where your love and devotion lie.

Once you obey out of love, God the Father will show His love to you. God the Son will show His love to you. And, with much love, God the Spirit will come to live in you. God's love and favor hinge on your choice of obedience. So what will you choose?

Lord Jesus, obeying You shows my love and acceptance of You. I pray I won't take my decision lightly.

YOUR CITIZENSHIP

Our citizenship is in heaven, and from it we await a Savior, the Lord Jesus Christ.

Philippians 3:20 ESV

When you're a citizen of a place, you know you belong. As a citizen you're offered protection, privilege, and responsibility.

When you commit your life to Jesus Christ as the Lord of your life, you gain citizenship in heaven. Until you fully realize your citizenship there by actually experiencing your heavenly home, you must wait to meet your Savior face-to-face.

But as you wait, don't forget that this earth isn't your forever home. You're not a permanent resident or citizen of wherever your earthly home is. Nevertheless, you can make the most of your time by serving God in this temporary residence while waiting for and wondering about your forever, heavenly home!

Lord Jesus, I'm waiting for You! I can't imagine what my heavenly home will be like, but I know You will be there! Thank You for the protection and privilege that comes with being a citizen of heaven!

MADE RIGHT

For our sake he made him to be sin who knew no sin, so that in him we might become the righteousness of God.

2 Corinthians 5:21 esv

Have you ever had to take someone else's punishment? Maybe you were wrongly accused and whoever actually misbehaved got away without any consequences. Suffering punishment that is not rightfully yours is not enjoyable, is it?

Most people wouldn't jump at the chance to receive someone else's punishment. In fact, it's typical to try to get out of punishment and consequences completely, even if you absolutely deserve them.

But Jesus is different. He came to earth on a rescue mission—specifically to rescue you from the punishment of your sin. That's pretty sacrificial, loving, and kind! As a result of His rescue, you're able to become the righteousness of God. That simply means you're made right with God through Christ.

Without Jesus, the punishment would be yours and you would be considered at odds with God. But with Jesus and His willingness to take your punishment for sins, you're made right with God!

Lord Jesus! Thank You for coming to rescue me. Thank You for taking my punishment so I could be made right with God.

HOW RICH?

My God will supply every need of yours according to his riches in glory in Christ Jesus.

Philippians 4:19 ESV

If you're a planner, you may feel frustrated when the future seems unclear. What will happen? What should you do? You might want to mentally map out the next phase of your life: Who will your friends be? What will happen after you graduate? When you're old enough to choose, where should you live? What should you do with your life?

These big questions are worth praying about and pondering. But keep in mind that no matter how sketchy the future may seem, God will supply every need of yours. Every need!

The wonderful truth is that God won't supply every need of yours with a bare minimum. He will supply your needs according to His riches in glory. Do you know how glorious God is? His wealth far surpasses money or jewels. Finances are no object to Him because He is Lord of absolutely everything. You can trust Him and rest when you're wondering about your future. He'll richly supply every one of your needs!

Father, You are so great!
Thank You for sharing Your wealth with me.

ALWAYS LEARNING

"And now I entrust you to God and the message of his grace that is able to build you up and give you an inheritance with all those he has set apart for himself."

Acts 20:32 NLT

Throughout your life, you'll meet many teachers. If you're blessed, you might even have a few mentors who help guide you in a wise, godly way. Yet as much as teachers and mentors are wonderful, they won't always be with you. At some point, because of life circumstances, they won't be such a big influence in your life.

Even without teachers, you still can and will be taught. In fact, God will find a way for you to keep learning. He will make a way to build you up. By using the truth of His Word and life experiences, He'll help you know and understand the message of His grace.

As you learn and experience more of God's grace throughout your life, you'll be built up in Him. As you're built up, it will be your turn to become the teacher and pass along His truth to others.

Father, please help me keep learning the message of Your grace. Please continue to build me up in You!

WAITING

For all creation is waiting eagerly for that future day when God will reveal who his children really are. Against its will, all creation was subjected to God's curse. But with eager hope, the creation looks forward to the day when it will join God's children in glorious freedom from death and decay.

ROMANS 8:19–21 NLT

Waiting isn't an easy thing. Especially if you tend to be impatient, it can feel really, really hard and frustrating to reach a milestone or wait for a big event like summer vacation.

Yet there's something even bigger all of creation is waiting for: the day when Jesus will return. All of creation will finally be freed from the effects of the fall of man. Nothing will decay anymore. Nothing will die. Creation will live in freedom, and just like Psalm 148 describes, every part of creation will praise the Lord.

Until that day, creation waits in hope. You can too!

Father, please help me wait patiently for Jesus' return. I can't imagine life without death or decay, but it sounds amazingly wonderful! What freedom!

PEACE THAT COMES THROUGH TRUST

You will keep in perfect peace those whose minds are steadfast, because they trust in you.

Isaiah 26:3 NIV

When you have a steadfast mind, you determine to be faithful, constant, and loyal. You can set your mind on anything—you might set your mind to work hard at school or determine to practice until a skill becomes second nature.

If you choose to set your mind on Christ and fully trust Him, worries of this world won't faze you. You'll know that God is in control of all so that you don't have to be concerned about what might happen. He has a plan, and you can walk confidently in it.

When you put your complete trust in Christ, you have an absence of worries and a sense of perfect peace. Your concerns fade as you experience a true peace you can't explain. All of that perfect peace comes as a result of your faithful trust in Christ.

Lord Jesus, I trust in You! I want to set my mind on You to experience peace. Besides, I know You are worthy of my complete trust!

IN THE MIDDLE OF THE MIRE

You, O Lord, are a shield about me, my glory, and the lifter of my head. I cried aloud to the Lord, and he answered me from his holy hill.

Psalm 3:3–4 ESV

Every person faces difficulties. You might be in a tough spot right now, where it seems like absolutely everything is going wrong. When you feel like you're in the middle of the storms of life, cry out to God! Tell Him every one of your complaints. Admit that you're weak or afraid or frustrated or mad. Tell Him all about your fears and feelings.

As you're honest with God, not only will He listen, but He'll also respond. He'll answer your prayers and protect you, just like a shield. He'll be your shining greatness in the middle of all the dark days of life. And He'll lift and hold your head high, just when you know you can't do it in your own power. Whenever you feel like you're stuck in the miry mud of life, call out to God. He will hear and He will help.

Father, thank You for being so kind and faithful to help me when I need You most!

CHANGES

Just as you accepted Christ Jesus as your Lord, you must continue to follow him. Let your roots grow down into him, and let your lives be built on him. Then your faith will grow strong in the truth you were taught, and you will overflow with thankfulness.

COLOSSIANS 2:6–7 NLT

When you accepted Christ Jesus as your Lord, a huge change happened: You stepped from death to life. The changes didn't stop at that moment; in fact, you'll change and grow the rest of your life.

As you continue to follow Christ, you'll learn more about Him and grow closer to Him. All the changes won't happen overnight. Instead, they'll be gradual in a process called sanctification. Being sanctified means you're in the process of being made holy.

Holiness comes as a part of following Christ. As you learn more and more of His truth, you can build your life on Him and establish deep roots in Him so your life won't be shaken. Your faith will grow stronger the longer you are part of Christ. To top off everything, your thankfulness will overflow!

Jesus, I want to keep learning from You and growing closer to You! Please help me become more and more like You.

STOP AND PRAY

Do not be anxious about anything, but in everything by prayer and supplication with thanksgiving let your requests be made known to God. And the peace of God, which surpasses all understanding, will guard your hearts and your minds in Christ Jesus.

Philippians 4:6–7 ESV

In this world, it can be easy to focus on anxious thoughts. Some people wear their worries and uneasiness like a badge and even brag about it by telling everyone, "I'm a worrier!" But you don't have to worry. In fact, the Bible tells you not to be anxious about anything. That's right—you can stop worrying!

When you're tempted to give in to your anxious thoughts, pray instead. As you pray, honestly tell God everything that's on your mind. As you thank God for what He has already done for you, His peace will come rushing to the scene and guard your heart and mind from worry. You won't be able to understand why or how it works, but when it does work, be sure to thank your heavenly Father!

Father, thank You for Your peace! I can't understand it, but I'm so thankful for the way it calms me down and guards my heart and mind.

ABSOLUTELY NOTHING

Who shall separate us from the love of Christ?
Shall trouble or hardship or persecution or famine or
nakedness or danger or sword? . . . No, in all these things
we are more than conquerors through him who loved us.

ROMANS 8:35, 37 NIV

Sometimes it seems like a lot of things in life could or should separate you from Christ's love.

Hardship could drive a wedge between you and Christ's love, right? No. Nothing can separate you from His love.

Facing troubles or being persecuted for your faith would put a strain on your relationship with Christ, right? No! Nothing can separate you from His love.

How about big troubles in life—like being so poor that you run out of food or clothing? Or what if natural disasters come and wipe everything away? Could those separate you from the love of Christ? No! Nothing can separate you from His love.

No matter what you face, you can always experience the never-ending love of Christ.

Jesus, thank You for loving me! The fact that absolutely nothing can separate me from Your love is a wonderful gift.

MY PLANS VERSUS GOD'S PURPOSE

Many are the plans in the mind of a man,
but it is the purpose of the Lord that will stand.

Proverbs 19:21 ESV

New Year's resolutions are really popular—if you set a bunch of goals at the beginning of a year, you supposedly can become way more effective in life than you currently are. The imagined success of New Year's resolutions seems enticing, but how many resolutions fizzle and fade away a couple of weeks after they're made?

It's easy to make plans and set goals and create resolutions, but they're really just well-intentioned wishes and dreams. What makes a difference? The purpose and plans of the Lord. Those are the plans that will succeed and actually happen.

But it's not as if your plans or hopes are bad—in fact, it's good to try to improve weak areas of your life. But instead of believing like they absolutely must come true, hold them with an open hand. Pray for the Lord's guidance and directions, make some goals or plans, then see if your plans end up being God's plans too!

Father, please give me direction and help me discern what could be good plans for my life.

SHOW IT!

I always thank my God as I remember you in my prayers, because I hear about your love for all his holy people and your faith in the Lord Jesus.

PHILEMON 4-5 NIV

Have you ever met someone who ended up completely surprising you? Maybe she acted one way or said certain things, and you were completely shocked to find out she was someone else.

Saying or acting one way and then revealing you believe something completely different isn't an authentic way of living. In fact, it's totally fake.

When you come to Christ in faith, it's time to authentically believe and respond with the way you speak and act and think.

Jesus told His followers to love others—fellow believers and holy people, but also people who don't believe in Him and are far from a Christian life. As you live a life of love, you'll show your belief and trust in Christ. You'll show you're serious about your relationship with Him. You'll show that your faith is authentic and the real deal.

Lord Jesus, I want to be known for my faith in You! Please help me love others the way You've asked.

SMILE!

Let all who take refuge in you be glad; let them ever sing for joy. Spread your protection over them, that those who love your name may rejoice in you. Surely, LORD, you bless the righteous; you surround them with your favor as with a shield.

PSALM 5:11–12 NIV

When you think about all the Lord has done for you and all you have through Him, you should be really glad and have a big smile on your face.

In the same way, you can be happy when you remember that God protects you and showers you with His favor! You can be really, truly glad to remember God is your safe place, and you can run to Him for shelter when it feels like your heart is breaking or you're scared.

Through Christ, you're made right with God. And with that *right-ness*, God begins to bless you. He won't only bless you, but He'll surround you with His favor. To know you're surrounded with God's favor? That's something to make you smile!

Father, thank You for Your really wonderful gifts! Thanks for surrounding me with Your favor! Thanks for protecting me! I want to be glad in You!

ENCOURAGED

May our Lord Jesus Christ himself and God our Father, who loved us and by his grace gave us eternal encouragement and good hope, encourage your hearts and strengthen you in every good deed and word.

2 Thessalonians 2:16–17 niv

Everyone needs encouragement. Even the most confident people in the world struggle with insecurity—they just might hide their feelings really well. But as uncertain as people might feel, encouragement does a wonderful job at silencing doubts.

Encouragement simply means to inspire with hope and courage. When you consider what Jesus did for you, you can feel full of His hope. He gives you courage to face this world until you're with Him for eternity.

The Holy Spirit can strengthen your spirit and encourage your heart, but you have to pay attention to how He does it. He may speak to you through God's Word or by what someone else says or does. He might encourage you through your circumstances or through an obvious blessing or answered prayer. Keep looking for the good that God is working in your life and feel encouraged. He is for you!

Lord, thank You for encouraging me. Help me keep my eyes focused on You and the many ways You're blessing me!

WHEN DISASTER STRIKES

"Though the mountains be shaken and the hills be removed, yet my unfailing love for you will not be shaken nor my covenant of peace be removed," says the Lord, who has compassion on you.

Isaiah 54:10 NIV

Nothing can seem to rock your world quite like a catastrophe. Natural disasters seem to bring the world to a screeching halt. Sickness can add a huge pause to your daily life. When tragedy strikes, all that's normal stops for a while.

In the middle of the worst moments of your life, remember that nothing changes the way God loves or cares for you. Nothing alters His eternal promises. He still is God; no circumstance changes the reality of who He is. No matter what, you can continue to trust and worship Him. You can continue to experience His love and His peace, even in your darkest days. When disaster strikes, God is still watching out for you!

Lord, I know that no one can escape awful days. When I'm faced with difficulties, please help me experience Your love and peace in very real ways.

PEACE

Let the peace that comes from Christ rule in your hearts. For as members of one body you are called to live in peace. And always be thankful.

Colossians 3:15 NLT

Peace feels so strange in this world. When everyone focuses on differences and picking sides of "right" and "wrong," peace seems impossible. When mean people gang up and bully others with actions or words, peace feels out of reach. When fear spreads and worries multiply, peace feels so otherworldly.

Peace won't happen in a worldly way where everyone will get along in total agreement. Peace is possible only through Jesus. As Jesus promised, "Peace I leave with you; my peace I give you" (John 14:27 NIV).

Without Christ, you'll never experience His peace. But with Christ ruling in your heart and your life, His peace that can't fully be understood or explained will guard your heart and mind. Because of His peace, you can live in peace with others.

Lord Jesus, You give me peace. Thank You! I know I need to let it rule in my heart. Please always calm my worries and my fears. May I trust in You and rest in Your peace.

GETTING STRONGER

*The Lord is my strength and my shield;
my heart trusts in him, and he helps me. My heart
leaps for joy, and with my song I praise him.*

Psalm 28:7 niv

If you've ever tried to become physically stronger, you know it doesn't happen instantly. It takes time and a lot of work and practice to build your muscles and grow stronger.

Just like your physical muscles, your spiritual muscles also need time, work, and practice to get stronger and stronger. Yet the more you trust in the Lord, the stronger you and your faith will become. When you trust Him, He will help you. He'll protect you like a shield, and He'll strengthen you to stand up against evil schemes and attacks.

Instead of taking God's strength and protection for granted, be sure to thank and praise Him for what He's doing in your life. And celebrate! It makes God happy to know that He's filling you with joy. The stronger you get, make sure you praise and celebrate even more.

Lord, I'm so glad You are my strength and my shield! I do trust You completely. Thank You for Your help and for filling me with joy.

PART OF A FAMILY

May the God who gives endurance and encouragement give you the same attitude of mind toward each other that Christ Jesus had, so that with one mind and one voice you may glorify the God and Father of our Lord Jesus Christ.

Romans 15:5–6 NIV

When you belong to Christ, you become part of His family—with countless other people who belong to Christ too. You're not alone. You have brothers and sisters in Christ. And just as in any family, it's important to treat each other with love and respect.

Sometimes you need to put a lot of effort into getting along with each other. Unity doesn't always come naturally. But it's still so important.

The good news is that God doesn't leave you on your own to figure things out. He gives you endurance and encourages you to become humble, loving, and kind, just like Jesus.

As you try to treat your brothers and sisters in Christ like you would like to be treated, you'll glorify God. When you're unified with other believers, pray, and try to be a good sister in Christ, you'll glorify God.

Father, I'm so glad I'm part of Your family! Please help me honor You in the way I treat my brothers and sisters in Christ.

HE LOVED ME FIRST

We love because he first loved us. If anyone says, "I love God," and hates his brother, he is a liar; for he who does not love his brother whom he has seen cannot love God whom he has not seen.

1 John 4:19–20 ESV

Love is woven throughout the entire Bible. God loved the world so much that He gave His only Son. And His Son, Jesus, taught and lived a life of love. He assured His followers that they needed to love so much that they'd be known for their love.

Love should be the trademark of every follower of Christ. You can love because God loves you. That love for others should overflow out of you because it's God's love. You don't have to love in your own strength or by your own will. Because God loved you first, you can love others in your life—whether they seem completely lovable or unlovable.

Lord, Your love for me is so amazingly wonderful and generous and never-ending. Thank You! I love You! Please help me show my love for You by loving others too.

THE STING OF REJECTION

The Lord says, "I was ready to respond, but no one asked for help. I was ready to be found, but no one was looking for me. I said, 'Here I am, here I am!' to a nation that did not call on my name. All day long I opened my arms to a rebellious people. But they follow their own evil paths and their own crooked schemes."

Isaiah 65:1–2 NLT

How do you feel when someone ignores you? Have you felt hurt? Rejected? Believe it or not, God knows how you feel.

Whenever people choose to overlook Him, refuse to give Him credit, or outright ridicule Him, God knows the hurt. Even when He faces rejection, God still opens His arms, ready to welcome people in. He calls out and is ready to be found.

Some people (hopefully *you*!) hear Him and come running, ready for His help and open arms. But others choose to ignore Him, rebel against Him, or outright reject Him. How do you choose to respond?

Lord, You are ready to be found. Thank You for being willing to face rejection just to save any and all who will turn and come to You.

KNOWN

O LORD, you have examined my heart and know everything about me. You know when I sit down or stand up. You know my thoughts even when I'm far away. You see me when I travel and when I rest at home. You know everything I do. You know what I am going to say even before I say it, LORD. You go before me and follow me. You place your hand of blessing on my head.

PSALM 139:1–5 NLT

Whether or not you believe it, you're a fascinating person. You may wish someone else took the time to get to know the real you with all your hopes, fears, strengths, and even weaknesses. What would be even better? If someone knew you completely and chose to love you.

Here's some amazing news: Your wish is granted. Someone *does* know every single detail about you and loves you completely. That special someone is your heavenly Father. He knows what you do and think and what you'd like to say before a word is even on your lips. Even if you can't fathom that He can absolutely know and love you, He does!

Father, it's amazing to realize how well You know me. And the fact that You love me too? Wow! I'm in awe.

NEVER CAST OUT

"All that the Father gives me will come to me,
and whoever comes to me I will never cast out. . . .
For this is the will of my Father, that everyone who
looks on the Son and believes in him should have
eternal life, and I will raise him up on the last day."

John 6:37, 40 ESV

It can be easy to imagine God with human traits. If humans are moody and change their minds, wouldn't God? But it's important to remember that humans are created in God's image. They reflect Him. God doesn't reflect humans.

Being saved from eternal separation from God and from getting the punishment you rightly deserve comes through faith in Christ. Once you truly believe and trust in Christ completely, eternal life is waiting for you. This is God's will and way.

You don't have to worry about God changing His mind every time you sin. You don't have to worry about whether your salvation is legit. God the Father knows all believers—He has chosen them and knows they'll come to Christ. When they do come to Him, they'll never be cast out.

Lord, I know I don't deserve eternal life,
but I'm so glad You've offered it to me through
Jesus! Thank You for choosing and calling me.

NOT YOUR OWN

You are not your own, for you were bought with a price. So glorify God in your body.

1 CORINTHIANS 6:19–20 ESV

Think about something that belongs to you. It might be something living, such as a pet, or it might be one of your favorite belongings you want to keep forever. It's easy to call that belonging your possession because it's yours. It's not its own—it belongs to you.

In the same way, Christ bought you at a great price: His very life. Because He paid such a costly price for you, you matter to Him. You belong not to yourself anymore but to Him. Since you're His valuable belonging, you should live like it.

Instead of pretending that you belong to yourself and can choose to do anything you please, remember the cost Christ paid. He suffered and died for you then defeated death so you could live forever with Him.

Start living in light of that truth right now. Make life choices that will make God happy. Glorify Him with your body. You have just one life and one body—use them to bring glory to your Lord!

Lord, please help me live in light of what You've sacrificed for me.

SELFLESS

Don't look out only for your own interests,
but take an interest in others, too.
Philippians 2:4 NLT

It can be really easy to stay self-centered and focus on what you like or what makes you happy. Do you feel comfortable? Do that! What do you feel like doing right now? Do that! Does this make you feel good? Do it!

But wait! Before you do what makes you happy, take a moment to stop and think. Many big issues come with being self-centered, and a major one is that being self-centered revolves around being selfish. When your focus is all about you and what brings you happiness and comfort, you tune out everyone else.

Christ calls us to be like Himself: loving, humble, and selfless. Instead of being selfish and centered only on what you're interested in, you can take a genuine interest in others too. When you do, you'll find that your heart grows as you consider others.

Lord Jesus, please help me to be more like You! I want to take my eyes off myself. Please help me look to You—and others!

NO ONE ELSE

For since the world began, no ear has heard and no eye has seen a God like you, who works for those who wait for him! You welcome those who gladly do good, who follow godly ways. But you have been very angry with us, for we are not godly. We are constant sinners; how can people like us be saved?

ISAIAH 64:4–5 NLT

Have you ever considered that there's not a single person or thing who is like God? No one else works for those who wait for Him like God does. No one else offers to forgive those who fall short of perfection and run into sin.

But God does. God made a way for the ungodly to be forgiven. He made a way for sinners to be saved. That way is through Jesus, who came to earth as the only Way, the only Truth, and the only Life. No one comes to the Father but through Him.

When you come to the Father through Jesus, your sins are forgiven. You're guaranteed a future in heaven. You don't have to worry about earning favor, because you've been given favor through Christ alone. No one else.

Jesus, I worship You! You are the Way, the Truth, and the Life, and I trust in You!

HOPE FOR THE WEARY

"I will satisfy the weary soul, and every languishing soul I will replenish."

JEREMIAH 31:25 ESV

Are you feeling weary right now? Are you worn out by the stresses of your day? You might have troubles at school or concerns about your family or drama with friends. When you stay focused on the world and your epic to-do list and ever-changing relationships, it's easy to feel worn out.

The antidote to weariness is spending time with your heavenly Father. Tell Him what's zapping your energy, strength, and thoughts. Be honest about your worries and what's exciting to you. Then get into His Word and see what He has to say. Spend time reading and pondering the truth of the Bible. Read just one verse and ask yourself what it says. What do you observe? What does it mean? How can you apply that one bit of scripture to your life right now?

As you spend time with the lover of your soul, you'll discover that He's the one who satisfies and replenishes your weary soul.

Father, I'm tired. I'm worn out. Please satisfy my weary soul and replenish the deepest part of me!

PRAYING FOR YOU

"I am praying not only for these disciples but also for all who will ever believe in me through their message. I pray that they will all be one, just as you and I are one— as you are in me, Father, and I am in you. And may they be in us so that the world will believe you sent me."

JOHN 17:20–21 NLT

Did you know that before Jesus faced the cross, He prayed specifically for you? His friend and disciple John detailed some of Jesus' final prayers, and Jesus prayed for *you*.

Wonder what He prayed about? He prayed that you'd be one with other believers. That means that living in unity with other Christ followers is really important. The world is full of division and differing opinions, but those who follow Christ have one major thing in common: their Lord!

The other thing Jesus prayed for you is that you'd be in the Lord. When you walk closely with Him and honor Him with your life, the world notices. Your life is a huge testimony that points to the truth of God.

Lord Jesus, it's amazing You prayed for me in Your last hours on earth. Please help me to be unified and honor You with my life!

ALL PRAISE

All praise to God, the Father of our Lord Jesus Christ, who has blessed us with every spiritual blessing in the heavenly realms because we are united with Christ. Even before he made the world, God loved us and chose us in Christ to be holy and without fault in his eyes. God decided in advance to adopt us into his own family by bringing us to himself through Jesus Christ. This is what he wanted to do, and it gave him great pleasure. So we praise God for the glorious grace he has poured out on us who belong to his dear Son.

EPHESIANS 1:3–6 NLT

Do you know what God has done for you through Christ? He has blessed you with every spiritual blessing. He has united you with Christ. He loved you even before He made the world. He chose you to be in Christ. He decided to adopt you, an outsider, into His own family. He brought you to Himself through Jesus.

Doing all of those things for you brought Him great pleasure. It should bring you great pleasure too! And it should fill your heart, mind, and mouth with praise. Praise God, the Father of your Lord Jesus Christ!

Father, I praise You! Thank You for choosing me and planning so many outrageously wonderful things for me. I worship You!

SCRIPTURE INDEX

OLD TESTAMENT

Genesis

Exodus

Deuteronomy

2 Kings

2 Chronicles

Esther

Psalms